Mollie
MAKES

WOODLAND FRIENDS

♡making ♡thrifting ♡collecting ♡crafting

CONTENTS

KNIT, SEW, CRAFT, CROCHET

MAKES FOR THE HOME

FUN CHARACTERS

GREAT GIFT IDEAS

WELCOME TO THE WOODS

The handmade world is a forest of foxes, owls, and acorns. Everywhere you look for inspiration, there's wood-grain print, cute critters, and antlers galore, so we're pleased to present our squirreled-away collection of nature-loving ideas from our favorite *Mollie Makes* designers.

Containing 18 knitted, stitched, crocheted, and papercrafted projects, *Woodland Friends* is our take on the trend—fresh and modern makes in our signature style, with a touch of quirk thrown in of course! Slow down for an evening or a weekend and discover how satisfying it is to create something for your home, as a gift, or just for you. Perhaps you'll dig out your sewing machine for Jane Hughes' gorgeous Woodland Walk Quilt or pick up your knitting needles for Hanna Hart's Flying Fox draft excluder—fun!

For the young (or young at heart), there's also Olívia Kovács' crocheted Forest Friends puppets and Mollie Johanson's Book Band Gang. Or throw a fun kid's party accessorized with napkin ring portraits of their favorite woodland creatures, thanks to Laura Howard's nifty how-to.

Choosing a favorite is tricky, so I'll go for two: Laura Fisher's cute-yet-plump Badger Pillow and Kirsty Neale's Foxy Sleep Mask. Well, who can resist that adorable snoozing face?

With step-by-step photographs and clear instructions, each of our projects is a breeze to follow. Our designers have even thrown in tried-and-tested tips to help you create your best project to date. Whether you're a beginner crafter or feel at ease adapting the instructions to suit you, our ethos is to give it a go and do it your way! Embrace wonkiness and imperfections; make it your own, and most of all, enjoy.

Here's to living and loving handmade ….

Lara

Lara Watson
Editor, *Mollie Makes*

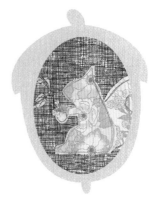

KAWAII-STYLE
FELT CRITTERS

THIS SWEET RACCOON AND HIS TINY FOX FRIEND MAKE GREAT GIFTS. THEY ARE CREATED BY HAND STITCHING LOTS OF LITTLE FELT SHAPES TOGETHER, WHICH IS A LITTLE FIDDLY BUT DEFINITELY WORTH THE EFFORT. SIMPLY ADD A RIBBON TAB TO PRESENT AS A KEY RING, OR SEW A BROOCH FINDING ONTO THE BACK TO BRIGHTEN UP A COAT LAPEL.

DELIGHTFUL
DUO

HOW TO MAKE ... FELT CRITTERS

TIP

These woodland critters have been made from a realistic palette of felts, but a brightly colored selection would look just as good. Why not use up your stash to whip up a few vibrant alternatives?

01 Use the templates provided to cut out two heads, two bodies, and two tails, from gray felt for the raccoon and from orange felt for the fox. Cut out two left and two right ears from black felt for the raccoon and from orange felt for the fox.

02 Cut out the small appliqué details as follows: from white felt, two snouts, one tail tip (fox only), four foot pads, and one belly (raccoon only); from black felt, two ear tips (fox only), two noses, one eye mask (raccoon only), one tail tip and the tail stripes (raccoon only), four front legs, and four back legs.

03 Take a head piece and stitch on the eyes, nose, and mouth details, remembering to add the eye mask for the raccoon; stitch the black tips to the top of the front pieces of the fox's ears. When stitching on the small felt components, you will find it easiest to use a sharp embroidery needle and sewing cotton or just one strand of embroidery thread.

04 Place a front and back ear piece together and sew around the edge, leaving the joined ear open at the base; fill with a little stuffing. Repeat to make the second ear.

05 Sandwich the ears between the front and back head pieces, and add a small piece of folded ribbon for the key ring tab. Blanket stitch around the edge, leaving open at the base of the head for attaching to the body later. Add a little stuffing.

06 Stitch the appliqué details to the front tail piece, then place it on top of the back tail piece, aligning the edges. Stitch all the way around the edge using a small blanket stitch, working with a thread that matches the color of your felt for a neat finish, and adding a little stuffing before completing the stitching.

07 Take one of your body pieces and line it up on the tail so that the tail sticks out at an angle from the desired side. Attach the body along the straight edge of the tail using backstitch. This becomes the back.

08 Now stitch the front and back body pieces together (stitching the raccoon's white belly to the front first), fill with stuffing and slip stitch all the way around the edge. Tuck the body into the head by approx ⅜" (1 cm), slightly tilting the head to one side and making sure there is sufficient stuffing wedged

inside. Stitch around the entire circumference of the neck with running stitch to secure.

09 Stitch (or glue) the back legs to the bottom edge, then add the white foot pads. Attach the back legs in the middle of the tummy to finish.

SEE PAGE 90 FOR TEMPLATES

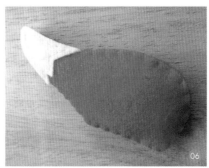

CHARLIE MOORBY
aka THE SAVVY CRAFTER

Charlie is a thrifty craft blogger and incurable stitching addict with a penchant for anything handmade. Commissioning Editor by day and crafter by night you'll find her collecting buttons and hoarding ribbons on a daily basis.
She's a dab hand with a pencil and loves a spot of cross stitching, too.
Find her online at
www.thesavvycrafter.com

EASY PIECE PATCHWORK

WOODLAND WALK QUILT

ALL THE THINGS YOU MIGHT JUST BE LUCKY ENOUGH TO SEE WHEN TREKKING THROUGH THE WOODS ON A CRISP FALL DAY INSPIRED THIS SUPER LITTLE QUILT. MEASURING APPROX 35" x 43" (89 x 109 CM), IT IS THE PERFECT SIZE FOR SNUGGLING UNDER ON THE COUCH WITH A GOOD BOOK, OR FOR DRAPING OVER A CHILD'S BED.

COZY
LAP QUILT

HOW TO MAKE ... WOODLAND WALK QUILT

MATERIALS

10 FAT QUARTERS OF QUILTERS' COTTON
IN A VARIETY OF NATURE-INSPIRED PRINTS

47" (119.5 CM) OF COTTON FABRIC
FOR BACKING

39" (99 CM) OF COTTON FABRIC
FOR BINDING

47" (119.5 CM) OF LIGHTWEIGHT QUILT WADDING

WHITE OR IVORY SEWING THREAD

STICKY NOTES AND PENCIL

PINS, SEWING NEEDLE, SCISSORS, AND IRON

SEWING MACHINE

ROTARY CUTTER, RULER, AND CUTTING MAT

TIP

A rotary cutter and cutting mat
makes quick work of cutting out
the fabric squares; if you don't
have these items, you can make
a card template and hand cut
the squares using scissors.

01 Cut 30 squares—three from each fat quarter—measuring 8" x 8" (20.5 x 20.5 cm) and press. Working on a clean floor, randomly place the squares to give you five rows across by six rows down, but avoid having the same pattern in any row. Label six sticky notes 1 to 6. Starting at the top left-hand corner, pin a number label on the first square of each row so all six rows are numbered. Carefully put each row of squares (in order) in a pile, with the numbered square at the top.

02 Piece the quilt top: using a 5/16" (8 mm) seam allowance, begin sewing the first row of squares together (keep the number pinned on). Sew the squares in the remaining five rows together to give you six rows of squares. Press seams open, then stitch the rows together one at a time, again with a 5/16" (8 mm) seam allowance; press the seams. Flip the quilt over, remove the number labels, then press the quilt top.

03 Lay the wadding flat on the floor. Place the pieced quilt on top (right side up); pin and cut away any excess wadding. Machine stitch together by top stitching 3/32" (2 mm) either side of all the seams.

04 Place the pressed backing fabric right side down on the floor. Lay your quilt on top and smooth flat. Pin and trim to size. Machine stitch through all layers close to the quilt edge, making sure they are straight.

05 To make the binding, cut five strips of fabric measuring 3" x 39" (7.5 x 99 cm). Stitch the strips together at a 45-degree angle and press flat. Press one of the ends of the joined fabric strip at a 45-degree angle, then press the binding strip in half.

06 Attach the binding with a 5/16" (8 mm) seam allowance beginning at X (see step 6 photo, top left). At a corner, sew almost to the edge; reverse stitch, and fold the binding upward (see step 6 photo, top right). Fold the binding back down (see step 6 photo, bottom left), turn the quilt, and continue. On the final side, stop 4¾" (12 cm) from the X; trim binding to leave a 1½" (3.8 cm) overlap and tuck this into the opening at the start. Continue stitching (see step 6 photo, bottom right).

07 To finish, pin the folded edge of the binding to the back of the quilt, mitering the corners neatly, then hand stitch the binding to the quilt.

JANE HUGHES

Jane from littleteawagon is
a crafter/designer with a fondness
for 70s fabrics and wallpapers,
making homewares and bags, and
blogging about a crafty life.
www.teawagontales.blogspot.com

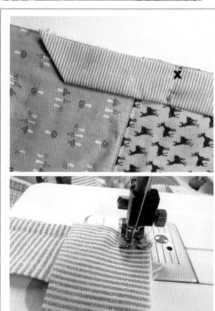

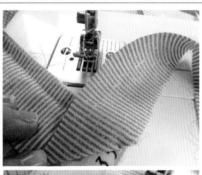

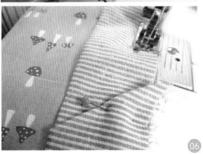

REVERSE APPLIQUÉ
MUG RUGS

THESE CUTE LITTLE PLACE SETTINGS MEASURE 8½" x 4½" (21.5 x 11.5 CM) AND ARE JUST THE RIGHT SIZE FOR A LARGE MUG AND A COOKIE OR TWO—IDEAL FOR YOUR COFFEE BREAK. THERE ARE FOUR FOREST FRIENDS TO CHOOSE FROM, EACH CUT IN NEGATIVE FROM YOUR TOP FABRIC TO REVEAL ITS SHAPE ON THE FELT FABRIC BENEATH—A TECHNIQUE KNOWN AS REVERSE APPLIQUÉ.

SWEET LITTLE PLACE MATS

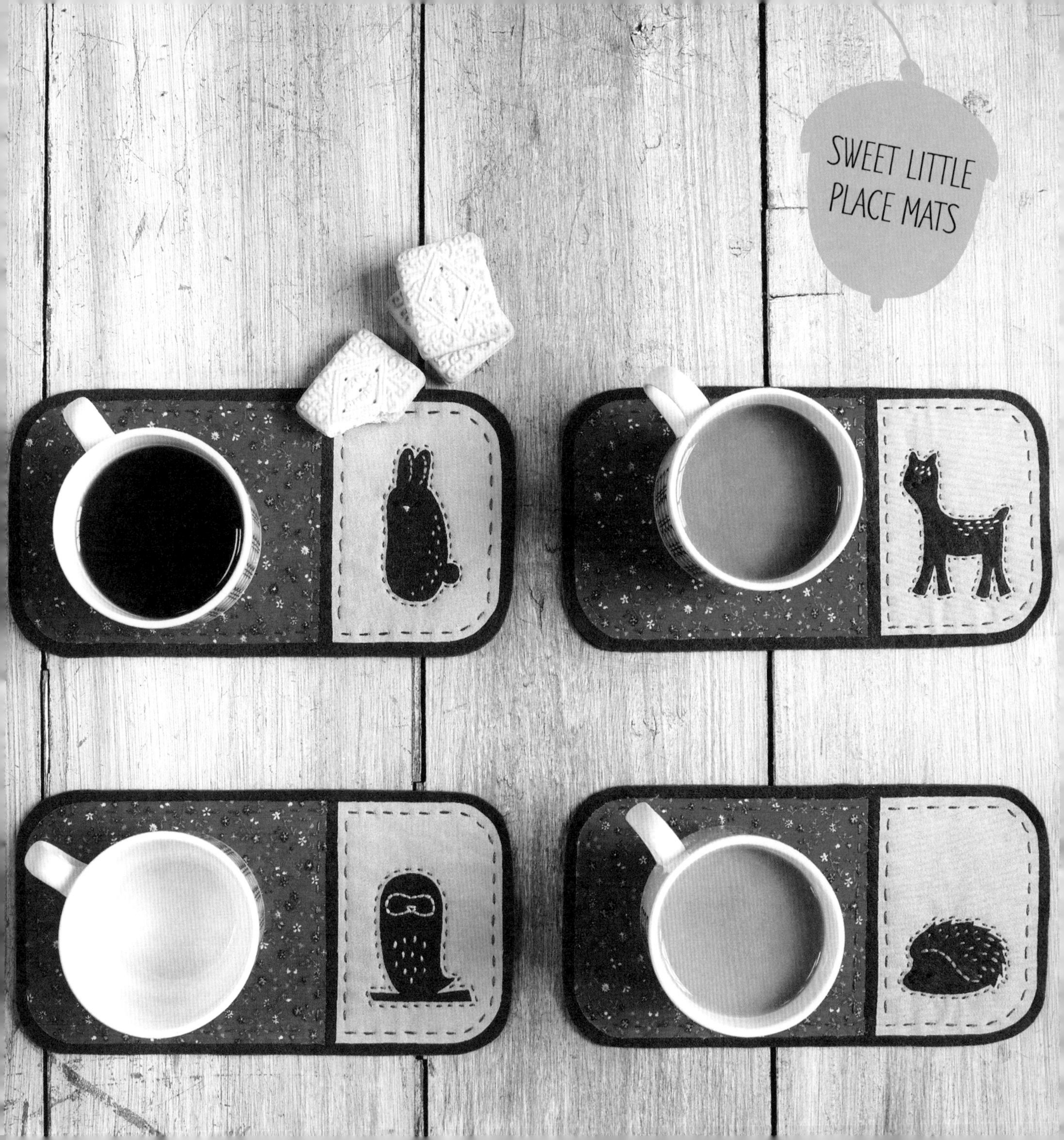

HOW TO MAKE ... MUG RUGS

SEE PAGE 90 FOR TEMPLATES

MATERIALS (PER MUG RUG)

ONE PIECE OF PRINTED FABRIC MEASURING
4½" x 5½" (11.5 x 14 cm)

ONE PIECE OF PLAIN FABRIC MEASURING
3½" x 5½" (9 x 14 cm)

TWO PIECES OF DARK BROWN WOOL-BLEND
FELT MEASURING 9" x 5" (23 x 12.5 cm)

ONE PIECE OF PAPER-BACKED FUSIBLE
INTERFACING MEASURING 9" x 10"
(23 x 25.5 cm)

EMBROIDERY FLOSS: WHITE, BLACK, LIGHT
BROWN, DARK BROWN, AND YELLOW

TRACING PAPER AND PENCIL

EMBROIDERY NEEDLE

SCISSORS

TIP

When choosing a printed fabric for the mug rug's larger section, look for colors and prints that are less likely to show tea or coffee stains: the mats should be spot cleaned or hand washed only.

01 Trace the two mug rug templates onto the paper side of the fusible interfacing. Taking the smaller mug rug section, trace a reversed outline of your chosen forest friend onto it. Iron the larger piece onto the printed fabric and the smaller piece onto the plain fabric, making sure that the fusible interfacing is glue side down. Cut out the mug rug sections, then carefully cut out the animal shape from the smaller section and discard.

02 Remove the paper backing from the large and small sections and position onto the felt so that the straight sides are next to each other with a small gap in between. Iron to fix in place.

03 Trace your chosen forest friend onto tracing paper, and hold it in front of the animal shape on the felt, lining up the outlines. Begin to work the embroidery details using three strands of embroidery thread.

04 For the rabbit, backstitch the ears and work the "fur" with lines of running stitch using light brown; satin stitch the nose in white. For the deer, use white running stitch to create the brow and back markings. For the hedgehog, use light brown for the backstitch face outline, then work

curving lines of running stitch for the spines. For the owl, use yellow thread to backstitch the face outline and to work the small stitches for the breast feathers.

05 Work French knots in black for the noses of the hedgehog and the deer and for all eyes. Once the embroidery is complete, carefully tear away the tracing paper.

06 Iron a piece of fusible interfacing to the back of the embroidered felt piece, then fuse to the second piece of wool felt to back the mug rug. Using three strands of dark brown embroidery thread, stitch a running-stitch border around each section of the mug rug and around the outline of the forest friend.

07 Trim off the brown felt around the outer edge, following the shape of the fabric pieces and leaving a margin of approx ¼" (6 mm).

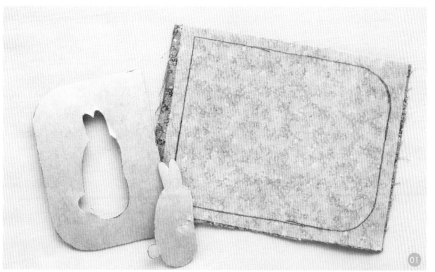

MOLLIE JOHANSON

Mollie Johanson began her blog Wild Olive as a creative outlet. Dreaming and doodling have resulted in embroidery and paper projects, most featuring simply expressive faces. Mollie lives near Chicago, commuting daily to her in-home studio via the coffee pot.
www.wildolive.blogspot.co.uk

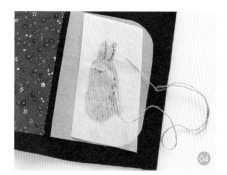

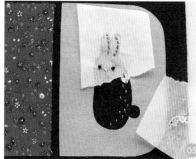

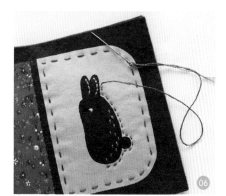

SILVER LEAF GARLAND

THIS SILVER LEAF GARLAND IS A STYLISH WAY TO BRING A TOUCH OF WOODLAND MAGIC INTO YOUR HOME AT CHRISTMAS TIME. YOU COULD STRING IT ALONG A MANTELPIECE WITH SMALL SPRIGS OF GREEN FOLIAGE AND RED BERRIES. FOR A PRETTY EASTER DECORATION, TRY MAKING THE LEAVES FROM PASTEL COLORS.

GREAT
HOLIDAY
DECORATION

HOW TO MAKE ... SILVER LEAF GARLAND

MATERIALS

PIECES OF THICK BROWN PAPER OR THIN CARD MEASURING 6" (15 CM) SQUARE

SHEETS OF SILVER LEAF

SIZE AND PAINTBRUSH

THIN WHITE CARD

TRACING PAPER AND PENCIL

SCISSORS

SPRING HOLE PUNCH AND CUTTING BOARD

STRING

TIP

The pieces of brown paper used are slightly bigger than the silver leaf sheets. Buy silver leaf sheets that have a backing, like a transfer, as these are easier to work with. To make a pretty gift tag, you could thread a single leaf onto ribbon.

01 Trace off the leaves and pine cone shapes and transfer them onto the sheet of thin white card. Carefully cut out the shapes and set them aside to use as your templates later.

02 Use the paintbrush to apply the size to your pieces of thick brown paper. Wait for 30 minutes for the size to get tacky, then lay down a silver leaf sheet on each piece of brown paper, rubbing the backing to adhere the silver to the size.

03 For a distressed effect, scrunch up a bit of paper into a ball and use it to rub all over the surface of the silver leaf to wear away some areas.

04 Turn the paper over and arrange some of your templates on the back. Draw around the templates and cut out the leaves and pine cone shapes. Repeat the process until you have as many shapes as you require: for example, to make a finished garland 72" (180 cm) long as shown, a total of 18 leaves and pine cones is required.

05 Make a crease down the center of each leaf, stopping at the stalk. To make the pine cone, fold diagonal lines across the shape approx ⅜" (1 cm) apart; turn and repeat to form creased box shapes.

06 Punch a hole in the center of the stalk of each leaf and pine cone.

07 Cut a 90" (230 cm) length of string and, allowing for approx 8" (20.5 cm) string at each end for hanging, tie the leaves and pine cones on along the length of the string allowing for a space measuring approx 4" (10 cm) in between.

SEE PAGE 91 FOR TEMPLATES

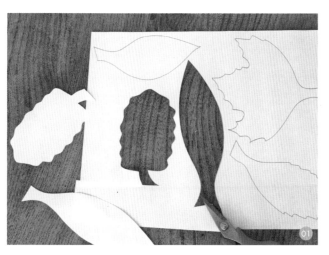

CLARE YOUNGS

Designer-maker Clare was given a craft book with a pile of paper and fabric at the age of eight and she hasn't stopped making since! Having trained as a graphic designer, she worked in packaging and illustration until turning to craft full time. Clare has written several craft books— to find out more, visit www.clareyoungs.co.uk

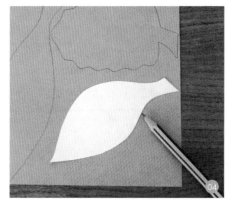

TISSUE BOX COVER

THE TISSUE BOX COVER IS MADE OF FOUR PANELS (SEE PAGE 27), EACH ONE FEATURING A FOREST DENIZEN: RABBIT, FOX, BEAR, AND DEER. EACH ANIMAL FACE IS CROCHETED SEPARATELY, THEN STITCHED ON. ROTATE THE BOX ANY TIME TO SHOW WHICHEVER CREATURE SUITS YOUR FANCY.

HOW TO MAKE ... TISSUE BOX COVER

MATERIALS

50G BALLS (196 YARDS/180 METERS) OF DROPS ALPACA, ONE EACH IN MEDIUM GRAY 517 (A), AQUA GRAY 7323 (B), DARK OLIVE 7238 (C), OLIVE 7233 (D), OFF-WHITE 100 (E), BROWN 401 (F), MEDIUM PINK 3720 (G), BLACK 8903 (H), RUST 2925 (I), LIGHT BROWN 607 (J), AND CAMEL BEIGE 302 (K), OR SIMILAR YARN (SPORT-WEIGHT 100% ALPACA)

SIZE B1 OR C2 (2.5MM) CROCHET HOOK

STITCH MARKER

TISSUE BOX TO COVER

EIGHT BLACK SEED BEADS FOR EYES

TWO ¼" (6 MM) BLACK BEADS FOR FOX AND DEER NOSES

BLACK SEWING THREAD

SEWING NEEDLE AND DARNING NEEDLE

TENSION TIP

22 sts and 29 rows to 4" (10 cm) over sc using B1 or C2 hook.

01 Make top panel of cover.

Note that all sc sts are made into back loop only of previous sc row; this creates a ridged effect.

Foundation row: Using yarn A, make 26ch.

Row 1: 1sc into second ch from hook, 1sc into each ch to end of row, turn. (25sc)

Rows 2–13: 1ch, 1sc into each sc, turn.

Make the right-hand side of the slot:

Rows 14–18: 1ch, 1sc in next 7sc, turn. Fasten off once row 18 is complete.

Make the left-hand side of the slot:

Reattach yarn to row 13, 7sc from

Adapting Size

The tissue box shown is rectangular rather than being a perfect cube: the dimensions are 4¼" (11 cm) wide, 4¾" (12 cm) long, and 4¾" (12 cm) high. You can adapt the pattern for slightly larger or smaller tissue boxes. If you have a different box size, shorten or lengthen the foundation chain. You might need to make a few attempts using different numbers of stitches to get the desired results.

TIP

As the loose yarn ends are on the inside of the cover where they will not be seen, there is no need to weave them in invisibly—just enough to secure the ends so the piece does not unravel.

end. 1sc in each of last 7sc of row, turn. Working on these 7sc only, make a further four rows.

Row 19: 1ch, 1sc in next 7sc, make 11ch (to bridge the gap over the slot), work 7sc into the sc of the right-hand part of the slot, turn.

Row 20: 1ch, 1sc in 7sc, 1sc in 11ch, 1sc in 7sc, turn. (25sc)

Rows 21–32: 1ch, 1sc in each sc, turn.

Fasten off.

02 Make four side panels.

The four side panels are worked in one piece. The spring and fall panels (gray-blue and olive-green backgrounds) are slightly narrower to form the shorter sides. All sc sts are made into back loop only of previous sc row; this creates a ridged effect.

Foundation round: Using yarn B, make 22ch. Fasten off yarn B, join yarn C, make 26ch. Fasten off yarn C, join yarn D, make 22ch. Fasten off yarn D, join yarn E, make 26ch. Join round with sl st.

Round 1: Fasten off yarn E and join

yarn B. 1sc in second ch from hook, 1sc in next 20 ch (21sc). Fasten off yarn B and join yarn C. 1sc in second ch from hook, 1sc in next 24 ch (25sc). Fasten off yarn C and join yarn D. 1sc in second ch from hook, 1sc in next 20 ch. (21sc). Fasten off yarn D and join yarn E. 1sc in second ch from hook, 1sc in next 24 ch (25sc). Sl st to join round.

Rounds 2–35: Changing colors as set out above, 1ch, 1sc in each sc to end of round, sl st to join round. Fasten off.

03 Make rabbit's face.
Use a stitch marker to indicate the start of the round.

Abbreviations

(US terms used throughout)
ch: chain
dc: double crochet
dec: decrease
rem: remain(ing)
rep: repeat
sc: single crochet
sl st: slip stitch
sp: space
st(s): stitch(es)
US/UK differences:
US sc (single crochet) = UK dc (double crochet)
US dc (double crochet) = UK tr (treble)

Round 1: Using yarn E, make a magic loop, work 9sc into the loop, draw the circle closed and join with sl st. Inc sts on each round as follows to make a circular piece:

Round 2: 2sc in each sc, sl st to join round. (18sc)

Round 3: [1sc, 2sc in next sc] to end of round, sl st to join round. (27sc)

Round 4: [2sc, 2sc in next sc] to end of round, sl st to join round. (36sc)

Round 5: [3sc, 2sc in next sc] to end of round, sl st to join round. (45sc)

Round 6: 1sc in each sc, sl st to join round.
Fasten off and weave in ends.

04 Make bear's face.
Use a stitch marker to indicate the start of the round.
Rounds 1–6: Work as for rabbit's face but using yarn F.
Round 7: 1sc in each sc, sl st to join round.
Fasten off and weave in ends.

05 Add details to the faces.
For bear's face, embroider two small circles for eyes using yarn E. For both rabbit's and bear's faces, sew on two black seed beads for pupils. For rabbit, using black sewing thread, sew a black circle around each eye to mark it out from the rest of the face. Make the noses:
Using yarn H for bear and G for

rabbit, make 2ch loosely. Yarn over hook, insert hook into second ch from hook, pull yarn through so you have 3 loops on hook. Yarn over hook and pull through latest loop. Rep until you have 13 loops on hook (make fewer sts if this starts to get awkward). Carefully pull yarn through all loops on hook. Insert hook into second ch of foundation ch and make 1sc. Fasten off. Using the end of your hook, push the yarn ends into the middle of the bobble (this both rounds out the nose shape and hides the yarn ends).

06 Make rabbit's ears (make 2).
Foundation row: Using yarn G, make 8ch (5ch for foundation row plus 3ch counts as 1dc).
Row 1: Work 1dc in fourth ch from hook, 1dc in next 2ch, 1sc in rem 2ch. (6 sts)
Round 2: Fasten off yarn G and join yarn E. Make 2sc in each st, 2sc in sp between 3ch and next st, then, working into other side of foundation ch, make 2sc in each ch. Join with sl st. Fasten off and weave in ends. Rep for second ear. Stitch ears to rabbit's face, leaving a gap of about 2 sts between the ears.

07 Make bear's ears (make 2).
Round 1: Using yarn H, make a magic loop. Work 10sc into the

loop, pull the circle closed and join with sl st.
Round 2: Fasten off yarn H and join yarn F. Make 2sc in each sc, sl st to join round. (20sc).
Fasten off and weave in ends. Rep for second ear. Stitch ears to bear's face, leaving a gap of about 6 sts between the ears.

08 Make fox's and deer's faces.
Using yarn I for fox and yarn J for deer, make 13ch.
Row 1: 1sc into second ch from hook, 1sc into each ch to end of row, turn. (12sc)
Rows 2–3: 1ch, 1sc in each sc, turn.
Row 4: 1ch, skip first st, 1sc in next 11sc, turn. (11sc)
Row 5: 1ch, skip first st, 1sc in next 10sc, turn. (10sc)
Row 6: 1ch, skip first st, 1sc in next 9sc, turn. (9sc)
Cont dec as set until 2 sts rem.
Row 14: 1ch, skip first st, 1sc in final sc. Thread yarn through rem st and fasten off.

09 Add details to the faces.
For both the fox and the deer, embroider two small circles for eyes using yarn E, then sew on two black seed beads for the pupils of the eyes. Sew on the larger black bead for the nose.

10 Make fox's ears (make 2).
Attach yarn E to top right corner of fox's face, 1 or 2 sts in from edge.
Row 1: Working into top row of fox's face, 1sc in next 3sc, turn. (3sc)
Row 2: 1ch, 1sc into each sc, turn.
Row 3: 1ch, skip 2sc, 1sc into final sc. (1sc)
Row 4: Thread yarn through rem st, fasten off and join yarn I. Work 1sc evenly around the sts of the inner ear. The final sc should be level with the edge st of the row below. Join with sl st to row below and fasten off. Rep on other side of head for second ear. Fasten off; weave in ends.

OLÍVIA KOVÁCS

Olívia is a Hungarian artisan who lives in Budapest. Her room is full of balls of yarn just waiting for crochet hooks to whip them into shape. To find out more, visit www.oliviakovacs.com

11 Make deer's ears (make 2).
Attach yarn E to right upper edge of deer's face.

Row 1: 3ch, 1sc into second ch from hook, 1sc into final ch, turn. (2sc)

Round 2: Fasten off yarn E and join yarn J. Make 1sc in every st, 1sc in sp between first and second sc, then, working into other side of row 1, make 1sc in each ch. Fasten off. Rep on other side of head to make second ear. Fasten off and weave in ends.

12 Make deer's antlers (make 2).
Foundation chain: Using yarn K, make 10ch.

First branch: Sl st into first 4ch of foundation ch.

Second branch: Make 4ch, sl st into first 3ch of 4ch, sl st into fifth ch of foundation ch.

Third branch: Make 4ch, sl st into first 3ch of 4ch, sl st into sixth ch of foundation ch. Sl st into rem ch of foundation ch.

Rep for second antler. Fasten off and sew antlers to head.

13 Make up tissue box cover.
Stitch each animal to its respective background panel. Sew the top of the cover to the four rectangles. You can use pins to hold the pieces together to help you while sewing.

CROSS STITCH

SQUIRREL HAND WARMERS

THESE NIFTY LITTLE HAND WARMERS HAVE BEEN DESIGNED FOR COLD WINTER
WALKS—45 SECONDS IN THE MICROWAVE IS ALL THEY NEED TO KEEP YOU NICE AND
TOASTY. ONE IS DECORATED WITH A SQUIRREL, THE OTHER WITH A GIANT ACORN,
WORKED IN BLOCK COLOR CROSS STITCH—IDEAL FOR NOVICE STITCHERS.

CROSS STITCH
STARTER
PROJECT

HOW TO MAKE ... SQUIRREL HAND WARMERS

MATERIALS

TWO PIECES OF 28-COUNT CREAM LINEN
OR EVENWEAVE FABRIC MEASURING
8" (20.5 cm) SQUARE

ONE PIECE OF CREAM COTTON BACKING
FABRIC MEASURING 8" x 47 ½" (20.5 x 120 cm)

EMBROIDERY FLOSS: CINNAMON (ANCHOR 351/
DMC 400); GINGER (ANCHOR 370/DMC 975);
NUTMEG (ANCHOR 365/DMC 3826)

10oz (250g) NATURAL GRAINS SUCH
AS PEARL BARLEY

TAPESTRY NEEDLE SIZE 24 OR 26

EMBROIDERY HOOP APPROX 6" (15 cm)

SMALL PAIR OF SHARP, POINTED SCISSORS

PENCIL

PINS AND SEWING NEEDLE

SEWING MACHINE (OPTIONAL)

01 Take one piece of evenweave or linen fabric and find its center by folding it in half horizontally and then vertically. These fold lines correspond to the arrows marked at the side of the charted designs (indicating the chart center) and will ensure that you work your design centrally on the fabric. Mark the center point with a pin or needle, and place the fabric in the embroidery hoop.

02 Cut a length of embroidery thread, separate three strands, and thread these through the tapestry needle. Working in rows from the center upward, stitch the squirrel pattern working from the chart on page 95. Each square on the chart represents one cross stitch; the color of the square indicates the thread color (see chart key). Each cross is stitched over two threads on linen or evenweave (see Working the Stitches, page 89).

03 When the top half is complete, turn the fabric upside down in the hoop and stitch the rest of the pattern in rows from the center as before.

04 Remove the fabric from the hoop and iron the embroidery face down over a towel (this will protect the stitches). Draw a line about 1⅛" (3 cm) outside the embroidered design and cut out the shape. Cut three duplicate shapes from the backing fabric.

05 Layer the four shapes with the embroidery second from the bottom facing up; pin together.

06 Sew a ⅜" (1 cm) seam around the shape, leaving open approx 3" (7.5 cm) along the straightest edge. Cut notches into the curves taking care not to cut into the seam.

07 Turn the sewn shape right way out through the gap in the seam and fill with approx 5oz (142g) of grains. Neatly hand sew the seam closed, folding in the seam allowances.

08 To complete the pair of hand warmers, repeat steps 1 to 7, this time stitching the acorn pattern from the chart on page 95.

VERY IMPORTANT
Only use 100% natural
fabrics and threads—
synthetics will melt
when heated.

SEE PAGE
95 FOR
CHARTS

SOPHIE SIMPSON
aka WHAT DELILAH DID

Sophie is the designer, writer, and
compulsive stitcher behind embroidery
business, What Delilah Did. A perpetual
dreamer and period-drama obsessive,
she most ardently wishes she'd been
born centuries ago. Her first book
Storyland Cross Stitch has recently
been published.
www.whatdelilahdid.com

01

02

03

04

05

07

FOREST FANCIES

FLORA
AND
FAUNA

01

Los Angeles-based designer Tina Rodas is the creative force behind Hi Tree, which specializes in woodland-themed children's décor and accessories. This little log pillow, with its machine-stitched wood-grain pattern, is a typical example of her super-cute designs. For more about her work visit www.hitree.com.

02

It is the aim of Dutch designer Ingrid van Willenswaard to find and make things that brighten the everyday. When she found these wooden toadstools on a market stall, she couldn't resist adding a little color, so she crocheted covers for them. Visit her blog where she has lots of DIY projects to inspire you: www.ing-things.blogspot.com.

03

Mister Finch, a self-taught textile artist, is inspired by nature to create his fantastic creatures, such as these beautiful butterflies, which he has created from vintage tablecloths and samplers.
To see more of Mister Finch's wondrous creations visit www.mister-finch.com.

CUTE CRITTERS

04

Shelley is the creative force behind Gingermelon, producing easy-sew patterns, such as the Woodland Stufflings, a sweet little owl, fox, and deer trio. She has some free patterns and tutorials to share on her blog: www.gingermelondolls.blogspot.ca.

05

This raccoon is the creation of Sofie Skein of Bonjour Poupette. Each of Sofie's animal models is individually sculpted—she uses the polymer like a painter uses a palette, custom blending to invent new colors and textures. For her latest designs visit www.bonjourpoupette.com.

06

Meet Stanley the squirrel, hand-knitted by Sara Carr, from a bright orange-red lambswool. The detailing for Stanley's face and tail are worked with hand embroidery. Other adorable characters created by Sara include Brian the bear, Monty the fox, and Alfred the owl; they can be found at www.saracarr.etsy.com.

NAPKIN RING PORTRAITS

THIS SET OF FOUR COLORFUL NAPKIN RINGS, DECORATED WITH SCALLOPED
FRAME PORTRAITS OF AN OWL, A FOX, A BEAR, AND A RACCOON, ARE
GUARANTEED TO ADD INSTANT CUTENESS TO YOUR DINNER PARTIES.
ALTERNATIVELY, THESE ANIMAL PORTRAITS WOULD MAKE WONDERFUL BROOCHES.

DINNER
PARTY FUN

HOW TO MAKE ... NAPKIN RING PORTRAITS

MATERIALS (PER SET OF FOUR)

ONE PIECE OF GRAY FELT MEASURING
2³/₄" x 3¹/₈" (7 x 8 CM)

ONE PIECE OF BROWN FELT MEASURING
3¹/₂" x 5" (9 x 12.5 CM)

ONE PIECE OF LIGHT BROWN FELT
MEASURING 2" x 2¹/₂" (5 x 6.5 CM)

ONE PIECE OF WHITE FELT MEASURING
3¹/₈" x 4" (8 x 10 CM)

ONE PIECE OF BLACK FELT MEASURING
2³/₄" (7 CM) SQUARE

ONE PIECE OF ORANGE FELT MEASURING
2³/₄" x 4" (7 x 10 CM)

SMALL PIECE OF DARK BROWN FELT

FOUR PIECES OF BRIGHTLY COLORED FELT
EACH MEASURING 8" x 9¹/₂" (20.5 x 24 CM)

SEWING THREADS IN COLORS TO MATCH FELT

EMBROIDERY FLOSS: BLACK, BROWN, AND
LIGHT BROWN

SEWING NEEDLE AND EMBROIDERY NEEDLE

PINS AND SMALL, SHARP SCISSORS

01 Use the templates provided on page 92 to cut out all the pieces needed for each animal appliqué in the quantities and colors marked on the template page. When a left-hand and a right-hand piece are required, for example for the ears, remember to flip the template over before cutting out the second shape. Cut out two small black circles for the pupils of each animal's eyes (no template provided).

02 For each napkin ring, take one of your brightly colored pieces of felt and cut from it two strips measuring 6¹/₈" x 1⅝" (15.5 x 4.3 cm) to make the ring, and one frame and one circle using the templates provided. Cut a second circle from another brightly colored piece of felt to form the background for the animal portrait.

03 Position the head and body of your chosen animal on the background circle (note: for the owl, the head

and body is one piece). Pin in place, then use matching sewing thread and small whip stitches to sew the piece(s) to the backing felt. Remove the pins.

04 Using the finished photograph as your guide, select the pieces that make up the first layer of the animal's face. One by one, sew this first layer of shapes into position using whip stitch and matching sewing threads.

05 Add the next layer of shapes with more whip stitching, again using matching threads, until all the pieces have been sewn in place.

06 Add the embroidery details to complete the bear, raccoon, and owl portraits using three strands of embroidery thread throughout. Using black thread and backstitch, sew on the smiles of the bear and the raccoon: use small stitches to help create natural-looking curves.

07 For the owl, sew the "feathers" with light brown thread, stitching single stitches on the top of the head and all over the body. Then use dark brown thread to sew long individual stitches radiating from each eye.

TIP

To cut out small circles for the pupils, first cut a small square of black felt, then slowly cut into it in a spiral motion to form a circle.

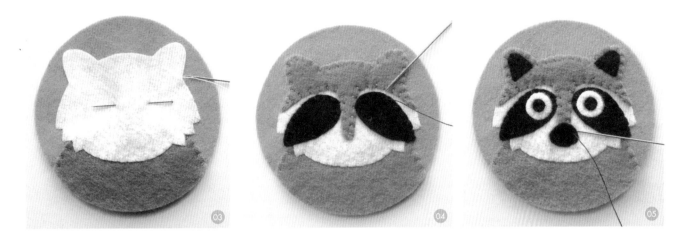

08 To make the napkin ring, pin the two strips of brightly colored felt together. Using blanket stitch and matching sewing thread, stitch together along the long edges, then remove the pins.

09 Bend the sewn-together strips to form a ring, overlapping the two short ends slightly. Using matching sewing thread, sew the ends together securely as follows: start in the center and sew a line of stitches out to one edge and back into the center, filling in the gaps between your stitches; repeat to complete the stitching in the other direction.

10 Take the two remaining unstitched shapes and place the circle in the center of the frame. Then place the napkin ring in the center of the circle, stitched edge down. Holding all three pieces together, turn them over and carefully sew the three layers together. Use matching sewing thread to sew a star shape, formed with six large stitches, in the center of the frame. Finish your stitching on the top of the frame where it will be hidden in the next step.

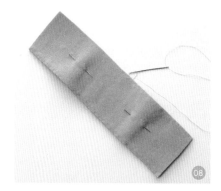

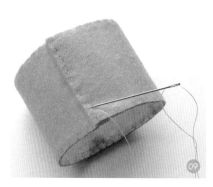

TIP

If you find blanket stitch a bit fiddly, you can use running stitch or whip stitch to sew the napkin ring strips together.

LAURA HOWARD aka LUPIN

Laura is a not-quite grown-up girl who likes to make and do and is completely obsessed with felt. She shares free tutorials and writes about her crafty adventures on her blog bugsandfishes.blogspot.com and sells her work at www.lupin.bigcartel.com

11 Position your animal portrait in the center of the scalloped frame and secure it with a couple of pins. Using sewing thread to match the frame and neat whip stitches, stitch around the edge of the circle. Your stitches should be worked through all three flat pieces of felt, to sandwich the scalloped frame in between the two circles.

12 Turn the napkin ring back and forth as you sew to check the placement of your stitches and to keep them neat on both sides. Finish your stitching neatly on the bottom circle, then remove the pins.

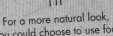

TIP

For a more natural look, you could choose to use four different shades of green for the napkin rings and circle/frames.

SEE PAGE 92 FOR TEMPLATES

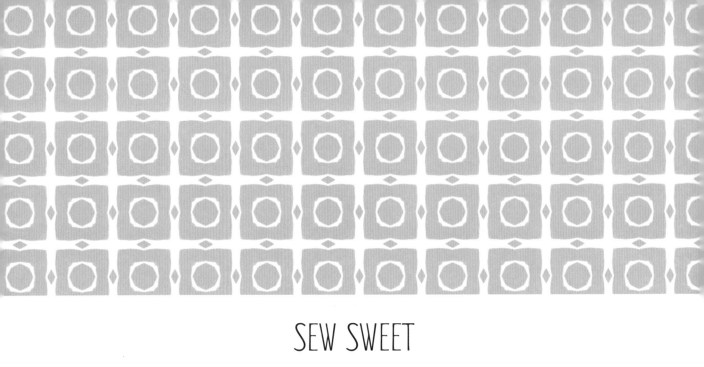

SEW SWEET

HEDGEHOG SEWING SET

THIS SWEET LITTLE SEWING SET INCLUDES A CUTE HEDGEHOG PIN
CUSHION, A LEAF-SHAPED NEEDLECASE TO KEEP YOUR SEWING NEEDLES
SAFE, AND LITTLE ACORNS TO ATTACH TO YOUR EMBROIDERY SCISSORS.
THE TWEED FABRICS USED PERFECTLY CAPTURE THE WOODLAND VIBE.

NEEDLE KEEP
AND PIN
CUSHION

HOW TO MAKE ... HEDGEHOG SEWING SET

MATERIALS

TWEED FABRIC: ONE PIECE FOR THE
HEDGEHOG'S BODY MEASURING 5" x 8"
(12.5 x 20.5 cm), ONE PIECE FOR THE LEAF
MEASURING 7" x 10" (18 x 25.5 cm),
AND OFFCUTS FOR THE ACORNS

ONE PIECE OF WOOL FABRIC FOR THE
HEDGEHOG'S HEAD AND BELLY MEASURING
6" (15 cm) SQUARE

ONE PIECE OF WADDING FOR THE LEAF
MEASURING 7" x 5" (18 x 12.5 cm)

EMBROIDERY FLOSS: DARK GREEN
AND BROWN

BLACK SEWING THREAD

TWO SMALL 4 mm BLACK BEADS FOR EYES

POLYESTER STUFFING

PINS, SEWING NEEDLE, AND LONG DOLL
SEWING NEEDLE

TIP
You can make several acorns as they look great hanging from your scissors or nestling in the leaf needle case.

01 To make the hedgehog pin cushion, use the templates provided to cut two bodies from the tweed fabric, and one belly and two heads from the wool fabric.

02 To make one side of the hedgehog, place together one head and one body piece and sew using a ¼" (6 mm) seam allowance. Repeat for the remaining head and body pieces to make the other side.

03 Pin the sides together right sides facing and stitch from nose to tail, leaving the bottom open for the belly piece. Pin the belly piece to the body/head, aligning the pointed end of the belly piece with the nose. Stitch together using a ¼" (6 mm) seam allowance and leaving a small opening along one side for stuffing.

04 Remove the pins, clip into the seams taking care not to cut the stitches, and turn right side out. Stuff the hedgehog with the polyester stuffing. To attach the bead eyes, thread the long doll sewing needle with black thread and take it through the stuffing opening to bring it out at the desired position on the face; thread on the bead for the first eye position, and exit on the other side to thread on the second

bead eye. Embroider the nose using small satin stitches before stitching up the stuffing opening neatly by hand.

05 To make the leaf needlecase, use the template provided to cut two leaves from the tweed fabric and one leaf slightly smaller from the wadding. Put the tweed fabric leaves right sides together, then place the

THERESIA COOKSON

Theresia is a self-taught craftivist with many years' experience and she has contributed to many magazines and books worldwide. She recently moved from the UK to Melbourne, Australia, and you can read more about her work and her adventures on her blog.
www.minoridesign.blogspot.com

wadding on top. Stitch the leaf layers together around the edges, leaving a small opening. Clip the curved edges carefully, turn the leaf inside out and stitch the opening closed. Use green and brown embroidery thread to backstitch the leaf details if you choose to. Fold the leaf in half and stitch 1" (2.5 cm) in from the end to make the leaf curve.

06 To make the acorns, use the templates provided to cut two bottoms and one top for each acorn.

07 Place the acorn bottom pieces together, right sides facing, and stitch around the edge leaving the top open; turn right side out. Sew gathering stitches around the top opening, stuff firmly, pull up (not too tightly) and sew closed. Sew a line of gathering stitches around the edge of the acorn top piece and pull up to leave an opening; stuff loosely, pull together and stitch closed.

08 Place the acorn top on the acorn bottom and attach with small zigzag stitches using dark green embroidery thread. To attach acorns together, use sufficient thread to enable you to sew out of the top of one acorn to stitch it to the next one.

SEE PAGE 91 FOR TEMPLATES

SEW FAUX
HAPPY LOG POUCH

KEEP YOUR JEWELRY SAFE AND SOUND IN THIS LITTLE CLOTH BAG WHEN OUT AND ABOUT ON YOUR TRAVELS. IT MEASURES 7" x 9" (18 x 23 CM) OPEN, BUT ROLLS UP TO A COMPACT 7" x 2¼" (18 x 5.5 CM). THE CORDUROY, COMBINED WITH SOME FAUX BOIS STITCHING, CREATES A TEXTURE THAT IMITATES A REAL WOOD LOG.

HOW TO MAKE ... HAPPY LOG POUCH

DESIGNED BY MOLLIE JOHANSON

MATERIALS

ONE PIECE OF BROWN CORDUROY FABRIC MEASURING 8" x 10" (20.5 x 25.5 CM)

TAN COTTON FABRIC: ONE PIECE MEASURING 8" x 10" (20.5 x 25.5 CM) AND ONE PIECE MEASURING 7½" x 19" (19 x 48.5 CM)

ONE PIECE OF COTTON WADDING MEASURING 7½" x 19" (19 x 48.5 CM)

TWO PIECES OF BROWN TWILL TAPE MEASURING 2¼" (6 CM)

EMBROIDERY FLOSS: TAN AND BLACK

TWO SEW-ON PRESS-BUTTON SNAPS

TRACING PAPER AND PENCIL

EMBROIDERY NEEDLE

SCISSORS AND PINS

SEWING MACHINE

01 Using the template provided, trace the happy log embroidery pattern onto tracing paper. Hold your tracing in front of the corduroy fabric ready to begin the embroidery, stitching through both the paper and the fabric. Using three strands of tan embroidery thread, chain stitch the wood grain. Using six strands of black embroidery thread, satin stitch the face. Carefully tear away the paper.

02 Sew one side of the press-button snaps onto each piece of the twill tape, then fold the tapes in half to form tabs. Sew the tabs along the bottom edge of the corduroy 2" (5 cm) in from the sides with the snaps facing up.

03 Pin the large piece of tan fabric to the wadding and quilt the pieces on a sewing machine. (When quilting the lining, you can mark evenly spaced lines with a disappearing ink marker, or continue the faux bois look inside with wavy quilted lines.)

04 Fold the quilted lining in half, right sides together, and pin. Sew along the two sides with a ¼" (6 mm) seam allowance. Take the second

piece of tan fabric (the backing) and pin to the embroidered front with right sides together to make the bag. Sew along the sides and bottom edge with a ¼" (6 mm) seam allowance leaving the top edge open; clip the corners.

05 Turn the bag right side out, then slide the lining inside. Roll the bag from the top down to determine where the second half of the snaps should go. Unroll, then sew the snaps on.

06 Fold under the top edges of the bag and lining (right sides facing) and pin along the edge.

07 Using three strands of embroidery thread, stitch along the top edge of the bag with running stitch. Remove the pins, stuff your pouch with treasures, roll up, and snap shut.

SEE PAGE 94 FOR TEMPLATES

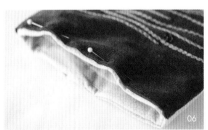

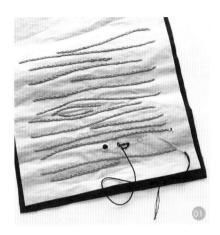

AMIGURUMI-STYLE
CROCHET SHELF ORNAMENTS

THESE LITTLE WOODLAND FRIENDS WOULD MAKE PERFECT ADDITIONS TO THE FAMILY, OR YOU CAN JUST ENJOY THEM AS DECORATIONS. SUPER-FUN AND SIMPLE TO CROCHET, THEY MAKE A WONDERFUL CRAFT PROJECT. EACH CREATURE IS ABOUT 5" (12.5 cm) HIGH AND ABOUT 6" (15 cm) LONG FROM PAWS TO TAIL.

HOW TO MAKE ... CROCHET SHELF ORNAMENTS

MATERIALS

TWO 50G BALLS (80 YARDS/73 METERS) OF BERNAT HANDICRAFTER COTTON IN SOFTLY TAUPE 13011 (A), OR SIMILAR YARN (WORSTED-WEIGHT COTTON)

70G BALLS (120 YARDS/109 METERS) OF LILY SUGAR 'N CREAM, ONE EACH IN WHITE 00001 (B) AND BLACK 00002 (D), OR SIMILAR YARN (WORSTED-WEIGHT COTTON)

ONE 100G BALL (210 YARDS/192 METERS) OF PATONS CLASSIC WOOL IN GRAY MIX 00224 (C), OR SIMILAR YARN (WORSTED-WEIGHT WOOL)

SMALL AMOUNT OF SENSATIONS ANGEL HAIR (120 YARDS/109 METERS PER 100G BALL) IN DARK BROWN 9715632 (E), OR SIMILAR YARN (WORSTED-WEIGHT WOOL AND SYNTHETIC MIX WITH FLUFFY TEXTURE)

SIZE G6 (4 MM) AND SIZE H8 (5 MM) CROCHET HOOKS AND STITCH MARKER

THREE PAIRS OF SIZE 18 MM BLACK SAFETY EYES

POLYESTER TOY STUFFING

TAPESTRY NEEDLE

01 Make the heads.
Round 1: Using G6 hook and yarn A for chipmunk, B for badger, or C for wolf, make 2ch, work 6sc into second ch from hook. (6sc)
Round 2: 2sc in each sc. (12 sc)
Round 3: [1sc, 2sc in next sc] until end. (18sc)
Round 4: [2sc, 2sc in next sc] until end. (24sc)
Round 5: [3sc, 2sc in next sc] until end. (30sc)
Round 6: [4sc, 2sc in next sc] until end. (36sc)
Round 7: [5sc, 2sc in next sc] until end. (42sc)
Round 8: [6sc, 2sc in next sc] until end. (48sc)
Rounds 9–13: 1sc in each sc.
Round 14: [6sc, sc2tog] until end. (42sc)
Round 15: [5sc, sc2tog] until end. (36sc)
Round 16: [4sc, sc2tog] until end. (30sc)
Round 17: [3sc, sc2tog] until end. (24sc)
For wolf and chipmunk, fix safety eyes 1" (2.5cm) up from working edge and 2" (5cm) apart (see step 5 for badger). Begin stuffing head.
Round 18: [2sc, sc2tog] until end. (18sc)

Round 19: [1sc, sc2tog] until end. (12sc)
Finish stuffing the head.
Round 20: Sc2tog until end. (6sc)
Fasten off, leaving a long end. With a tapestry needle, thread end through rem sts to gather up.

02 Make chipmunk's black eye stripes (make 2 lots).
Piece 1: Using G6 hook and yarn D, make 8ch; fasten off, leaving long end.
Piece 2: Make 2ch and fasten off, leaving long end.

03 Make chipmunk's white eye stripes (make 4).
Using G6 hook and yarn B, make 15ch; fasten off, leaving long end.

04 Attach chipmunk's eye stripes.
Take one of the longer black pieces, thread a tapestry needle with the yarn end and position the chain against the middle of the eye, slanting diagonally upward. Sew on the length of chain.

TENSION TIP
Tension is not important for this project, as long as the crochet fabric is good and dense so the toys can be stuffed firmly.

Rep with shorter black piece, placing it diagonally down from other side of eye. Rep on second eye. Take a white chain and fit it against the longer black chain. Press it against the head so that it is right next to the black chain and eye (see photo). Sew all the way down to fix in place. Rep on opposite side of eye, then rep for second eye. Fasten off and weave in ends.

04

05 Make badger's eye patches (make 2).
Round 1: Using G6 hook and yarn D, make 7ch, work 6sc starting at second ch from hook.
Round 2: 1ch to turn, 1sc in each sc.
Rounds 3–4: Rep round 2.
Round 5: 1ch to turn, 1sc, sc2tog twice, 1sc. (4sc)
Rounds 6–9: Rep round 2.
Round 10: 1ch to turn, 1sc, sc2tog, 1sc. (3sc)
Round 11: Rep round 2.
Round 12: 1ch to turn, 1sc, sc2tog. (2sc)
Round 13: 1ch to turn, sc2tog. (1sc)
Fasten off, drawing yarn through rem st and leaving a long end to sew with. Fix a safety eye in the middle of the bottom corner of the patch (see photo). Rep with second eye on other patch. Position patch diagonally on face and stitch in place. Rep with other patch, spacing the sharpest corners about 1½" (4cm) apart. Fasten off and weave in ends.

06 Make the muzzles.
Round 1: Using G6 hook and yarn A for chipmunk or B for badger and wolf, make 2ch, work 6sc in second ch from hook.
Round 2: 2sc in each sc. (12sc)
Rounds 3–4: Sc in each sc.
Fasten off, leaving a long end. Using a short piece of yarn D, sew long horizontal stitches on the upper part of the muzzle to form the noses (sew two lines for chipmunk and wolf and three for badger). For wolf, sew two vertical lines to form a T-shape. Then stuff the muzzles. With a tapestry needle, thread end through rem sts to gather up. Position each muzzle on the lower part of the head between the eyes, and stitch around the base. Fasten off and weave in ends.

07 Make wolf's fangs.
Using G6 hook and yarn B, make 3ch, dc2tog working first dc in second ch from hook. Rep for second fang. Fasten off, leaving a long end. Taking one fang, thread tail through a tapestry needle. Pass needle up through the bottom of the muzzle, coming out of the

05

CAPRI HULSEY
aka LITTLE BITTY KNITTER

Capri Hulsey and her parakeet Kiwi live out west underneath the desert stars in Arizona. Her love of both animals and of fiber arts fueled a hobby that quickly grew into a passion. To see more of Capri's work, visit www.littlebittyknitter.etsy.com, or check out her latest creations on Facebook.

TIP
Most of the pieces are worked in the round without slip stitching to join rounds. The stitch marker is used to indicate the first stitch in each round.

other end of the fang to attach it.
Rep for fang on other side of muzzle.
Fasten off and weave in ends.

08 Make chipmunk's ears (make 2).
Round 1: Using G6 hook and yarn A,
make 2ch, work 6sc in second ch from
hook, join round with sl st.
Round 2: Work 2sc in each st, join
round with sl st. (12sc)
Fasten off, leaving a long end.
Sew one ear to the top of the head,
lining it up with the eye stripes. Rep
with second ear on opposite side of
head. Fasten off and weave in ends.

09 Make badger's ears (make 2).
The ears will look like circles with a
slice taken out rather than a full circle.
Round 1: Using G6 hook and yarn
D, make 2ch, work 8dc in second ch
from hook, sl st to join round.
Row 2: 2ch, 2dc in next 6dc. (13 sts)
Fasten off, leaving a long end. Sew
one ear to the top of the head, lining
it up with the eye triangle. Rep with
second ear on opposite side of head.
Fasten off and weave in ends.

10 Make wolf's ears (make 2).
Round 1: Using H8 hook and yarn
B, make 2ch, work 4sc in second ch
from hook.
Round 2: 2sc in each sc. (8sc)
Round 3: [3sc, 2sc in next sc] twice.
(10sc)
Fasten off yarn B and join yarn C.

Rounds 4–5: Sc in each sc.
Round 6: [4sc, 2sc in next sc] twice.
(12sc)
Round 7: [5sc, 2sc in next sc] twice.
(14sc)
Fasten off, leaving a long end. Take
one ear, press flat, and sew together
at the edges. Sew ear to top of head
at an outward angle. Rep with second
ear on opposite side of head. Fasten off
and weave in ends.

11 Make the bodies.
Round 1: Using G6 hook and yarn A
for chipmunk, D for badger, or C for

wolf, make 2ch, work 7sc into second
ch from hook.
Round 2: 2sc in each sc. (14sc)
Round 3: [1sc, 2sc in next sc] until
end. (21sc)
Round 4: [2sc, 2sc in next sc] until
end. (28sc)
Rounds 5–8: Sc in each sc.
Round 9: [2sc, sc2tog] until end.
(21sc)
Round 10: [1sc, sc2tog] until end.
(14sc)
Stuff the bodies. Fasten off, leaving
a long end. With a tapestry needle,
thread end through rem sts to gather
up, fasten off, and weave in ends. For
each animal, take the head piece and
place it directly on top of the body
piece. Stitch the two together.

12 Make the feet (make 2).
Round 1: Using G6 hook and yarn A
for chipmunk, D for badger, or B for
wolf, make 2ch, work 6sc into second
ch from hook.
Round 2: 2sc in each sc. (12sc)
Round 3: [1sc, 2sc in next sc] until
end. (18sc)
Rounds 4–6: Sc in each sc.
For wolf, fasten off yarn B and join
yarn C after round 4. Begin stuffing
the legs.
Round 7: [1sc, sc2tog] until end.
(12sc)
Finish stuffing the legs.
Round 8: Sc2tog until end. (6sc)
Round 9: Sc in each sc.
Fasten off, leaving a long end. With a
tapestry needle, thread end through rem

sts to gather up. Place one foot toward the bottom of the body and stitch it in place. Rep with other foot, spacing the feet about 1" (2.5cm) apart. Fasten off and weave in ends.

13 Make the arms (make 2).
Round 1: Using G6 hook and yarn A for chipmunk, D for badger, or B for wolf, make 2ch, work 6sc into second ch from hook.
Round 2: [1sc, 2sc in next sc] until end. (9sc)
For wolf, fasten off yarn B and join yarn C.
Round 3: Sc in each sc.
Round 4: [1sc, sc2tog] until end. (6sc)

Abbreviations

(US terms used throughout)
ch: chain
dc: double crochet
dc2tog: double crochet two stitches together (decrease by one stitch)
rem: remaining
rep: repeat
sc: single crochet
sc2tog: single crochet two stitches together (decrease by one stitch)
sl st: slip stitch
st(s): stitches
US/UK differences:
US sc (single crochet) = UK dc (double crochet); US dc (double crochet) = UK tr (treble)

Rounds 5–7: Sc in each sc.
Stuff the ball-like part of the arm. Fasten off, leaving a long end. With a tapestry needle, thread end through rem sts to gather up. Place the top of the arm near the top side of the body, then sew the top of the arm in place. Fasten off and weave in ends.

14 Make chipmunk's tail.
Round 1: Using G6 hook and yarn E, make 2ch, work 5sc in second ch from hook.
Round 2: 2sc in each sc. (10sc)
Round 3: [1sc, 2sc in next sc] until end. (15sc)
Rounds 4–8: Sc in each sc.
Round 9: [3sc, 2sc2tog] until end. (12sc)
Rounds 10–11: Sc in each sc.
Round 12: [2sc, sc2tog] until end. (9sc)
Rounds 13–14: Sc in each sc.
Stuff the tail. Fasten off, leaving a long end. With a tapestry needle, thread end through rem sts to gather up, then sew bottom and middle part of the tail to the back of the body. Fasten off and weave in ends.

15 Make badger's tail.
Round 1: Using G6 hook and yarn D, make 2ch, work sc in second ch from hook.
Round 2: 2sc in each sc. (12sc)
Round 3: [2sc, 2sc in next sc] until end. (15sc)
Rounds 4–6: Sc in each sc.
Round 7: [2sc, sc2tog] until end. (12sc)
Round 8: Sc in each sc.

Round 9: [1sc, sctog] until end. (8sc)
Round 10: Sc in each sc.
Round 11: [Sc2tog] until end. (4sc)
Stuff the tail. Fasten off, leaving a long end. With a tapestry needle, thread end through rem sts to gather up, then place tail at base of lower back area, sewing all around the base to attach it.

16 Make wolf's tail.
Round 1: Using H8 hook and yarn B, make 2ch, work 4sc in second ch from hook.
Round 2: 2sc in each sc. (8sc)
Round 3: [3sc, 2sc in next sc] twice. (10sc)
Round 4: [4sc, 2sc in next sc] twice. (12sc)
Round 5: [1sc, 2sc in next sc] until end. (18sc)
Fasten off yarn B and join yarn C.
Rounds 6–8: Sc in each sc.
Round 9: [1sc, sc2tog] until end. (12sc)
Round 10: [4sc, sc2tog] twice. (10sc)
Round 11: Sc in each sc.
Stuff the tail, fasten off, and attach as the badger's tail.

PAPER PATCHWORK
STAG HEAD

CARDBOARD TROPHY STAG HEADS LOOK STUNNING IN A CONTEMPORARY INTERIOR AND ARE NOT DIFFICULT TO MAKE. THIS ONE IS COVERED IN A PATCHWORK OF PAPER SCRAPS AND ANYTHING CAN BE USED FROM WRAPPING PAPER AND WALLPAPER, TO STAMPS AND OLD MAPS. USE THE ANTLERS TO HANG UP YOUR JEWELRY.

STYLISH
JEWELRY
HOLDER

HOW TO MAKE ... STAG HEAD

MATERIALS

11¾" x 16½" (A3 SIZE) SHEET OF GRAYBOARD CARD EITHER 2 MM OR 3 MM THICK

PAPER SCRAPS FOR DECORATING

SMALL PIECE OF RIBBON FOR HANGING

TRACING PAPER AND PENCIL

CRAFT KNIFE, CUTTING MAT, AND METAL RULER

GLUE STICK

STRONG QUICK-DRYING GLUE

TIP
The grayboard can be substituted with foam board, which you may find easier to cut. When selecting your decorative papers, it is best to stick to a few colors and choose scraps that fit in with this palette.

01 Using the templates provided, trace out the shapes and transfer them onto the card sheet. You will need one set of antlers, one nose piece, two side pieces, and two backing pieces (one with and one without slots).

02 Working on a cutting mat, cut out the marked shapes with a craft knife, using a metal ruler for the straight edges. Be careful when cutting thick card: always make sure the blade is sharp so that it does not slip, go slowly, and keep the fingers of your other hand well out of the way. When cutting the slots, make them 1 mm wider than the thickness of the card you are using; for example, if you are using 3 mm thick card, make your slots 4 mm wide.

03 Cover the outside edges of the side pieces with small pieces of paper, overlapping the edges. Play around with different color combinations first, then when you are happy with the arrangement, stick them down with the glue stick.

04 Turn the covered pieces over and trim off any excess up to the edge of the cardboard. You must also remember to cut out the slots if they have been covered up.

SEE PAGE 94 FOR TEMPLATES

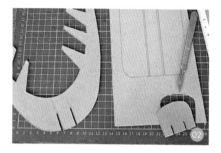

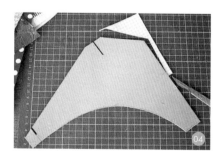

05 Cover the insides of the side panels with a single piece of paper (as you will only see a little of the inside of the panels, it is not necessary to spend time patching them).

06 Continue following steps 3–5 to cover the nose (both sides), the antlers (front only), and the backing piece with the slots in (front only).

07 Slot the nose into the slots at the front of the side panels, making sure they push fully into each other. If you find that they are a bit tight, you can trim a tiny sliver of card from the slots. Slot the antlers into the slots at the top of the side panels, making sure that you push them right into each other.

08 Cut a piece of ribbon approx 4" (10 cm) long. Fold it in half and secure it with a piece of tape to the center top of the undecorated backing piece (without slots) with the raw edges pointing down, to give you a ¾" (2 cm) hanging loop. Use the strong quick-drying glue to stick the decorated backing piece (with slots) on top, decorated side uppermost, sandwiching the ribbon in between.

09 Run lines of strong quick-drying glue in the slots and place the stag head into the slots; hold in position for a couple of minutes to let the glue dry a little. When the glue has fully dried, hang the assembled stag head on your wall.

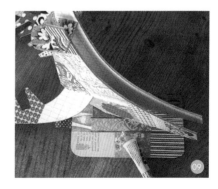

DESIGNED BY CLARE YOUNGS

CHARACTER KNIT

FLYING FOX

A DRAFT EXCLUDER IS A PRACTICAL SOLUTION TO HELP BANISH THOSE WINTER CHILLS, BUT WHO SAID IT CAN'T BE FUN? THIS FLYING FOX IS 35½" (90 CM) LONG EXCLUDING ITS TAIL, AND 12" (30 CM) AROUND. YOU CAN EASILY ADJUST THE LENGTH TO FIT YOUR DOOR BY KNITTING THE BODY LONGER OR SHORTER: SIMPLY ADD OR SUBTRACT 10 ROWS FOR EVERY 2" (5 CM).

CHARMING HOME ACCESSORY

HOW TO MAKE ... FLYING FOX

MATERIALS

TWO 100g BALLS (322 YARDS/295 METERS) OF STYLECRAFT DOUBLE KNIT SPECIAL YARN IN COPPER 1029 (A), OR SIMILAR YARN (DK WEIGHT ACRYLIC), USED DOUBLE THROUGHOUT

SMALL AMOUNTS OF DK WEIGHT YARNS IN BLACK (B) AND WHITE (C)

ONE PAIR OF SIZE 7 (4.5 mm) KNITTING NEEDLES

SIZE 7 (4.5 mm) CROCHET HOOK

SHEET OF 4oz (100g) WADDING 35½" (90 cm) LONG AND 54" (137 cm) WIDE (SHEET IS ROLLED INTO A CYLINDER BEFORE STUFFING)

TWO 12 mm SEW-ON TOY EYES

TWO STITCH HOLDERS

DRESSMAKING PINS

TAPESTRY NEEDLE

TENSION TIP

16 sts and 21 rows to 4" (10cm) square over st st using size 7 needles.

01 Make the body and head.
Start knitting from the tail end. Using yarn A, cast on 40 sts. Work in st st until body is 31½" (80 cm) long, ending with a purl row.
K30, put the last 10 sts on a stitch holder, turn.
P20, put the last 10 sts on another stitch holder, turn.
Carry on knitting with middle 20 sts.

02 Shape the head.
Start counting the rows.
Cont in st st, dec by 1 st (k2tog on RS rows, p2tog on WS rows) at beg and end of rows 1, 3, 5, 7, 9, 11, 14, and 17. (4 sts)
Row 18: Fasten off yarn A and join yarn B for nose. Cont in st st.
Row 22: [P2tog] twice. (2 sts)
Row 23: K2tog and draw yarn through rem st to fasten off.
Place the 10 sts from first and 10 sts from second stitch holder on a knitting needle. Knit the underside of the head the same as the upper side but using yarn A only. Fasten off.

03 Make the legs (make 4).
Using yarn A, cast on 11 sts.
Work in st st until leg is 4" (10 cm).
Fasten off yarn A and join yarn B.
Cont in st st for a further 2¾" (7 cm).
Bind off all sts. Fasten off.

Using yarn A, stitch three long vertical lines to form toes.

04 Join the leg seams.
Fold the leg RS together, placing the long seam in the middle. Sew end seam. Turn RS out. Sew seam along the leg. You can use pins to hold the piece together while seaming.

05 Make the tail (make 2 pieces).
Using yarn A, cast on 9 sts.
Working in st st, inc by 1 st (M1) at

HANNA HART aka MISS SNOWBERRY

Hanna lives in Dorset, where she designs and makes knitwear, bags, brooches, and home accessories. She has Scandinavian roots, and that heritage influences her designs. You can find her work at www.misssnowberry.etsy.com

beg and end of RS rows 7, 15, 23, and 31. (17 sts)

Cont in st st, dec by 1 st (k2tog) at beg and end of rows 45 and 49. (13 sts)

Row 51: Fasten off yarn A and join yarn C. Dec by 1 st (k2tog) at beg and end of rows 53, 55, 57, 59, and 61. (3 sts)

Row 63: K3tog and draw yarn through rem st to fasten off. Pin the two pieces RS together. Crochet around edge using single crochet (sc) stitch and single strand of yarn. Switch between yarns A and C to make seam in appropriate color.

06 Make the ears (make 4 pieces). Using yarn A, cast on 8 sts. Work in st st.

Row 3: Dec 1 st (k2tog) at beg and end of row. (6 sts)

Row 6: Fasten off yarn A and join yarn B.

Rows 8 and 10: Dec 1 st (p2tog) at beg and end of row. (2 sts)

Row 11: K2tog and draw yarn through rem st to fasten off. Pin the two pieces of each ear RS together and sew around edges.

07 Assemble the back end. Weave in all ends. Fold the end of body RS together placing tail and legs inside. Pin the pieces together and stitch back seam. Turn RS out.

08 Assemble the front end. With WS together, sew both sides of the head together. Position the front legs pointing slightly forward and stitch on underneath the body. Position the ears and eyes to give your fox a nice expression and sew in place.

09 Stuff with wadding. Roll up the sheet of wadding to a circumference of 11½" (29 cm) and cut off any excess. Tack the long edge to prevent the wadding from unrolling. Put the roll of wadding inside the knitted cover, placing a little extra wadding in the nose. Stitch up along the stomach.

Abbreviations

(US terms used throughout)

beg: beginning
cont: continue
dec: decrease
inc: increase
k: knit
k2tog: knit 2 sts together (dec by 1 st)
k3tog: knit 3 sts together (dec by 2 sts)
M1: make 1 (inc by 1 st)
p: purl
p2tog: purl 2 sts together (dec by 1 st)
rem: remain(ing)
RS: right side
st(s): stitch(es)
st st: stockinette stitch
WS: wrong side

HIS 'N' HERS
HOTTY BOTTY COVERS

SNUGGLE UP ALONGSIDE YOUR LOVED ONE WITH THESE MATCHING HOT WATER BOTTLE
COVERS MADE FROM SUMPTUOUS VELVET FOR EXTRA COZINESS. EACH IS APPLIQUÉD WITH
A FABRIC SILHOUETTE—FOR HER A STRIDING MOOSE AND FOR HIM AN AMBLING BEAR.
THE SIZE OF THE COVERS CAN BE EASILY ADAPTED TO FIT YOUR HOT WATER BOTTLES.

HOW TO MAKE ... HOTTY BOTTY COVERS

SEE PAGE 93 FOR TEMPLATES

MATERIALS

TWO PIECES OF VELVET FABRIC MEASURING 9³/₄" x 19¹/₄" (24.5 x 48.5 CM)

PRINTED FABRIC: TWO PIECES MEASURING 9³/₄" x 19¹/₄" (24.5 x 48.5 CM) AND ONE PIECE MEASURING APPROX 6" (15 CM) SQUARE FOR THE APPLIQUÉ

TWO PIECES OF WADDING MEASURING 9³/₄" x 19" (25 x 48.5 CM)

ONE PIECE OF FELT MEASURING APPROX 6" (15 CM) SQUARE

FUSIBLE WEBBING

1¹/₈ YARDS (1 METER) VELVET RIBBON

19³/₄" (50 CM) COTTON LACE TRIM (FOR HER COVER ONLY)

SEWING THREAD

CUTTING MAT, RULER, AND ROTARY CUTTER

SCISSORS

PENCIL AND PAPER

IRON AND COTTON IRONING CLOTH

SEWING MACHINE

01 If your hot water bottle size differs (see tip), make a pattern for cutting your fabric pieces by laying the bottle on a piece of paper and adding 1³/₈" (3.5 cm) to each side and the bottom, and 6" (15 cm) to the top.

02 To make the motif, iron fusible webbing to the wrong side of the small printed fabric piece. Using the template provided, cut out your motif from the fabric. Peel off the fusible webbing backing and iron the motif onto the felt, using the cotton ironing cloth to protect the felt. Iron a piece of fusible webbing to the wrong side of the felt. Carefully cut around the fabric motif to leave a few millimeters of felt showing around the outline, and peel off the backing.

03 Place the felt-backed motif onto one of the velvet fabric pieces so the animal's feet are approx 4¼" (11 cm) from the

TIP
The quantities given are for a cover measuring 7" x 11¾" (18 x 30 cm). Use a ³/₈" (1 cm) seam allowance throughout.

bottom (short) edge; iron to attach. Machine stitch around the motif just inside the edge of the printed fabric: go slowly and lift the presser foot to turn the fabric leaving the needle in the down position each time you do so.

04 Place a piece of wadding on the wrong side of the decorated velvet fabric, then place these two fabric layers on top of one of the large printed fabric pieces with right sides together. Making sure that the motif is facing the right way up (with the head end toward the top seam that you are about to sew) sew across the top edge. Unfold and press the seam over a cotton cloth.

05 To make the cover back, make a fabric sandwich as in step 4 with the remaining three pieces of velvet fabric, wadding, and printed fabric,

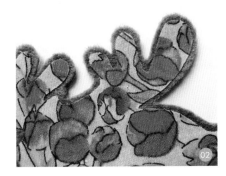

ensuring that the velvet pile is going the same way on both the front and the back of the cover. For her cover only, lay the lace on the lining fabric next to the seam and stitch in place.

06 With the front and back cover pieces unfolded, place together right sides facing and matching seams. Pin very well and sew around the edges, leaving an opening in the lining (printed fabric) for turning. Trim the seams, turn right side out, and sew the opening closed. Push the lining inside the cover making sure to push it into the corners.

07 Pop your hot water bottle inside the cover. Pin the center point of the ribbon to the back cover where you can feel the bottle's neck. Remove the bottle and stitch the ribbon in place.

08 Replace the hot water bottle, fold down the top to make the cuff and tie the ribbon in a bow.

JOOLES of SEW SWEET VIOLET

Jooles, a lover of sewing, craftiness, and eating cake, lives in West Sussex with her husband and her two gorgeous teenagers.
A homebody, she loves nothing more than a day spent in her sewing room pootling away. For her blog see sewsweetviolet.blogspot.com or discover more of her work at www.notonthehighstreet.com/ sewsweetviolet

WOODLAND WONDERS

01

These foxy fingerless mitts are just one of several woodland creatures available in the original animal fingerless glove collection at the Etsy shop, Pomber. These fun designs are created by Hungarian Olívia Kovács. You can see the full range at www.oliviakovacs.com.

02

This cute "wall art" embroidery kit from Penguin & Fish creator Alyssa Thomas comes with all the tools and materials you will need to get started with your embroidery. For more of Alyssa's quirky characters, available as kits, patterns, and fabrics, visit www.penguinandfish.com, or read her blog at www.penguinandfish.blogspot.com.

03

Designer/maker Samantha Stas trained as a graphic designer but has long since moved over to fabrics. A lover of all things vintage, she makes friendly fox collars that can be worn 100% cruelty-free, as they are made from a thick wool/mix felt and lined with pretty cotton fabric. Read Samantha's blog at www.samanthastas.blogspot.com.

DARLING
DEER

04

Texan-born Jordan Strickland Morris
currently lives and works in Kansas City
selling handmade clothes, jewelry, and
housewares under the name Hide the
Good Scissors. Her "Doe a dear" is
just one of several of her embroidery
designs influenced by her love of
geometric abstractions. You can find
out more about Jordan and her work at
www.jordanstrickland.com or drop by
her blog at www.hidethegoodscissors.
blogspot.com.

05

Taking inspiration from nature and the
forest, Edinburgh-based designer Kirsty
Anderson creates accessories and little
pieces of artwork with a fantastical, yet
old-time, feel under the label A Wooden
Tree. A vintage enthusiast, she breathes
a new lease of life into fabrics reclaimed
from granny's linen closet to create
wonders like the amazing Mr Stag.
www.awoodentree.com.

FELT EMBROIDERED
BOOK BAND GANG

THINGS YOU MIGHT PICK UP ON A WOODLAND WALK INSPIRED THESE CUTE CHARACTERS.
THE SIMPLE-TO-EMBROIDER FELT MOTIFS DECORATE BANDS OF ELASTIC USED TO HOLD
A NOTEBOOK TOGETHER OR TO KEEP YOUR PLACE AS A BOOKMARK. THEY ARE FUN TO
USE AND MAKE A PERFECT ADDITION WHEN GIVING A BOOK AS A GIFT.

INSPIRED BY FOREST FINDS

HOW TO MAKE ... BOOK BAND GANG

SEE PAGE 92 FOR TEMPLATES

MATERIALS (PER BOOK BAND)

THREE PIECES OF FELT IN DIFFERENT COLORS, EACH MEASURING AT LEAST 3" x 3¾" (7.5 x 9.5 CM)

EMBROIDERY THREADS IN COLORS OF YOUR CHOOSING

19¾" (50 CM) OF ⅜" (1 CM) WIDE ELASTIC (AMOUNT MAY VARY DEPENDING ON SIZE OF BOOK)

EMBROIDERY NEEDLE

TRACING PAPER AND PENCIL

SCISSORS

SCALLOP-EDGE SCISSORS OR PINKING SHEARS

01 Trace your chosen forest find motif onto a small piece of tracing paper. Hold the tracing paper motif on top of one layer of felt, and stitch through the paper and felt. Use six strands of embroidery thread to backstitch the outlines and three strands to stitch the face, working French knot eyes and backstitch detailing. When the embroidery is complete, carefully tear away the paper.

02 Cut around the embroidery, leaving a margin of about ¼" (6 mm). Place the embroidered motif on a second layer of felt and cut around the shape with scallop-edge scissors or pinking shears. Repeat to cut a slightly larger piece from the third felt color using regular scissors this time.

03 Measure the elastic around a book, stretching it a bit and allowing 1" (2.5 cm) of overlap. Cut the elastic to size.

04 Fold the largest piece of felt in half lengthwise and cut two small slits, just large enough for the elastic to fit through. Slide the elastic through the slits.

05 Place the other two layers of felt on top of the base layer and use three strands of embroidery thread to stitch around the design with running stitch to hold the layers together, being careful not to stitch through the elastic. Secure with a hidden knot.

06 Stitch the ends of the elastic together. If sewing by hand, be sure to use lots of stitches to make sure it is securely stitched. Slide the overlapping ends behind the felt embellishment for a neat finish.

TIP

If you are having difficulty sourcing colored elastic, you can use fabric dyes to color white elastic any shade you wish to.

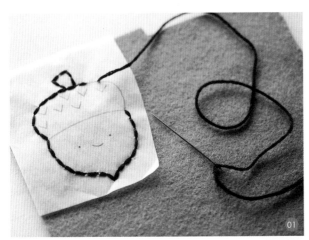

TIP

To make headbands instead of book bands, cut the slits in the other direction and size the elastic accordingly.

DESIGNED BY MOLLIE JOHANSON

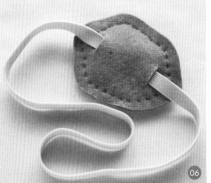

ANIMAL PICTURES

THIS COLLECTION OF WOODLAND ANIMAL PICTURES IS INGENIOUSLY FRAMED IN DIFFERENT-SIZED EMBROIDERY HOOPS. THE THREE APPLIQUÉ MOTIFS—A FAWN, A SQUIRREL, AND A MOUSE—ARE CUT FROM RETRO FABRICS. THEY WOULD LOOK GREAT HANGING TOGETHER ON A WORKROOM WALL OR IN A CHILD'S NURSERY.

GREAT FOR RETRO FABRICS

HOW TO MAKE ... ANIMAL PICTURES

MATERIALS

THREE PIECES OF PLAIN/TEXTURED FABRICS IN DIFFERENT COLORS MEASURING 9³/₄" (25 CM) SQUARE, 12" (30 CM) SQUARE, AND 15³/₄" (40 CM) SQUARE FOR BACKGROUNDS

SMALLER PIECES OF RETRO PATTERNED FABRICS FOR THE APPLIQUÉ

¹/₂ YARD (0.5 METER) OF PLAIN LIGHT COLORED COTTON FABRIC FOR BACKING

¹/₂ YARD (0.5 METER) OF FUSIBLE WEBBING

THREE WOODEN EMBROIDERY HOOPS: 5" (12.5 CM), 7" (18 CM), AND 9³/₄" (25 CM) IN DIAMETER

SEWING THREADS IN THREE DIFFERENT COLORS

EMBROIDERY THREADS

DOUBLE-SIDED TAPE

EMBROIDERY NEEDLE, SCISSORS, PINS, AND PENCIL

SEWING MACHINE AND IRON

01 Trace and cut out the three animal templates, including the additional details. Choose retro patterned fabrics for the animals (you will need two fabrics for the squirrel appliqué as the body and tail are cut separately) and cut out the pieces a little larger than your templates. Cut pieces of fusible webbing a little smaller than the templates and iron (without steam) onto the reverse of your chosen fabrics, then peel off the backing paper.

02 Pin an animal template to the right side of one of the fusible-webbing backed fabrics and cut out. Repeat for all three animals, making sure to cut the squirrel's tail in a different fabric from the body. Take some smaller scraps of retro patterned fabric, iron on fusible webbing, and use to cut out the small picture details.

03 Take your three background fabrics and press to remove any creases. Lay the fabrics out in a row. Cut three pieces of the plain light colored cotton fabric to the same size and set aside. Place the three hoop frames over the top of the fabrics, and then arrange your animal appliqués into position, including the small picture details. When you are happy with

the layout of each, remove the hoops and carefully take each background fabric piece to the ironing board—one at a time—to iron your appliqué pictures into place.

04 Now sew the appliqués in place with machine stitch, starting with the fawn picture. Using your sewing machine on a small stitch setting, start sewing around the edges of the fawn. Do this two or three times to give a defined line. Change thread color and repeat the process with the hearts. With the third thread color, stitch the toadstool.

05 Machine stitch the squirrel and mouse appliqués in the same way. To add the mouse tail, lightly draw on the shape first with a pencil using the template as a guide, before stitching on. To complete the mouse, satin stitch the nose using embroidery thread.

SEE PAGE 91 FOR TEMPLATES

01

02

03

06 Frame the finished appliqués in the relevant sized hoop. Take the hoop and remove the inner circle. Put double-sided tape all around the outside edge of the inner circle and place flat down on the work surface. Lay the correct-sized light colored fabric pieces over the inner circle. Place the appliquéd fabric on top, making sure that the picture is centered within the circle. Now take the outer hoop and push into place.

07 Making sure the fabric is stretched flat, tighten up the screw at the top to secure. Turn over and neatly trim off any excess fabric at the back.

04

05

DESIGNED BY JANE HUGHES

06

07

3D FELT
BADGER PILLOW

BRING A TOUCH OF SWEET WOODLAND CHARM TO YOUR HOME WITH THIS
ADORABLE BADGER PILLOW MEASURING 10" x 8" (25.5 x 20.5 CM). MADE OF
FELT, THIS DESIGN IS SIMPLE ENOUGH TO FINISH IN AN AFTERNOON, AND CAN
EVEN BE STITCHED BY HAND IF YOU DON'T HAVE A SEWING MACHINE.

CHARACTER CUSHION

HOW TO MAKE ... BADGER PILLOW

SEE PAGE 93 FOR TEMPLATES

MATERIALS

TWO PIECES OF BLACK FELT MEASURING 12" x 9" (30.5 x 23 CM)

ONE PIECE OF WHITE FELT MEASURING 4" x 6" (10 x 15 CM)

TWO BLACK 12 MM SAFETY EYES WITH WASHERS

ONE BLACK 15 MM SAFETY NOSE WITH WASHER

POLYESTER TOY STUFFING

SEWING THREADS: WHITE AND BLACK

SHARP, POINTED SCISSORS

SEWING NEEDLE AND PINS

SEWING MACHINE (OPTIONAL)

TIP
The finished pillow measures 10" x 8" (25.5 x 20.5 cm), but the templates can easily be enlarged to make a really big badger pillow.

01 First decide if you want your badger to face left or right; I chose to have mine facing right. Using the templates provided, cut the following shapes from your felt fabrics: two black bodies, one white face, and one right and one left white ear.

02 Pin the white face shape to one of the black body shapes so that the top of the face lines up with the top of the head, centering it between the ears. Pin the white ear shapes onto the black body as shown, centering them about 1" (2.5 cm) from the edge.

03 Using white thread, machine stitch the face and ears to the body (or you can stitch by hand).

04 Use sharp-tipped scissors to pierce small holes for the safety eyes and nose, making the holes only as wide as the shank for the plastic pieces. Insert the eyes and nose and fasten with the washers.

05 Match up the front and back body pieces with right sides facing, and pin together. Using black thread, sew around the edge with a ⅜" (1 cm) seam allowance, leaving a small opening approx 3" (7.5 cm)

along one of the straight parts of the body. Trim excess fabric around the seam and clip small notches into the curved areas, taking care not to cut into the seam. This will help reduce bulk and make for a smoother shape at the curves.

06 Turn the badger right side out and gently push out the shapes of the ears and feet with the eraser end of a pencil. Begin adding the stuffing, starting with the area farthest from the opening. To avoid lumps in the finished piece, it is best to fill slowly, using small handfuls of stuffing. Flip the badger over periodically while stuffing to check both sides for any signs of unevenness.

07 Once your badger is stuffed to your liking, slip stitch the opening closed with black thread doubled on the needle for a secure seam. You can add a little bit more stuffing as you stitch so that the badger is uniformly filled.

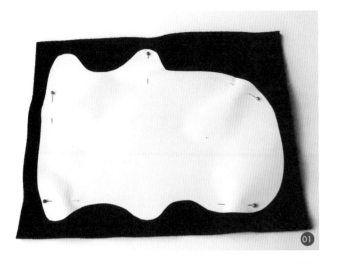

01

02

LAURA FISHER

Laura is a recent college grad, living in California, who loves creating things that make people smile. She enjoys being a handmade artist because of how fulfilling it is to see an idea come to life.
Find her online at
www.fluffedanimals.etsy.com

03

04

05

06

EASY SEW
FOXY SLEEP MASK

GET YOUR BEAUTY SLEEP AND LOOK EFFORTLESSLY FOXY AT THE SAME TIME WITH THIS FUN FELT AND PRINTED FABRIC MASK. IT CAN BE STITCHED BY HAND (OR MACHINE IF YOU PREFER), BUT BE SURE TO CHOOSE A SUPER-SOFT WOOL FELT SO THAT IT IS COMFORTABLE TO WEAR FOR AN AFTERNOON NAP.

CATCH
40 WINKS

HOW TO MAKE ... FOXY SLEEP MASK

SEE PAGE 91 FOR TEMPLATES

MATERIALS

TWO PIECES OF ORANGE PRINTED FABRIC MEASURING 10" x 6" (25.5 x 15 CM)

ONE PIECE OF WHITE FELT MEASURING 12" (30.5 CM) SQUARE

SMALL PIECES OF BLACK AND PALE PINK FELT

EMBROIDERY THREADS: WHITE, BLACK, AND PALE PINK

1 YARD (1 METER) NARROW RIBBON

SEWING THREAD AND NEEDLE

WATER-ERASABLE FABRIC PEN

SCISSORS AND PINS

IRON AND IRONING BOARD

TIP

Instead of ribbon ties, use a strip of elastic to keep the sleep mask in place: cut a strip to fit snugly around your head, and pin the ends to each side before stitching the layers together.

01 Trace the upper head template onto the reverse of one of your printed fabric pieces. Cut it out very roughly, leaving 1⅛" (3–4 cm) all the way around. Pin to the second piece of printed fabric with right sides facing. Sew around the outline to join the two pieces together, leaving a gap at the top edge for turning.

02 Trim the excess fabric to leave a ⅜" (1 cm) hem all the way around. Clip into the corners and along the curved edges to ease the seams.

03 Turn the upper head the right way out through the gap, and press the seams to neaten. Slip stitch the opening closed.

04 Using the templates provided, cut two heads from your two pieces of white felt, and two white inner ears, two pink cheeks, and a black nose from your felt scraps. Draw eyes onto one of the head pieces using the water-erasable fabric pen. Use black embroidery thread to stitch over the outline of each eye.

05 Place one pink cheek section on each side of the face, lining up the lower edges. Sew in place with small whip stitches, leaving the lower edges open for now. Sew a white inner ear onto each side of the printed fabric upper head section.

06 Cut two 15¾" (40 cm) lengths of ribbon and pin one end of each piece to either side of the head. Place the two white felt head pieces together, so the ribbon ends are sandwiched in between, then add the printed fabric upper head on top. Sew neatly along all edges to join the pieces securely together, using threads to match the fabrics.

07 Finally, stitch the black felt nose into place, and add approx seven French knots to either side to represent the whiskers.

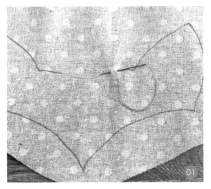

01

04

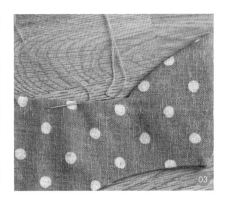

02

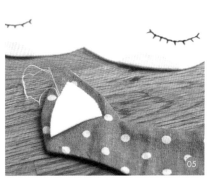

05

03

KIRSTY NEALE

Kirsty is a freelance writer and designer-maker. She specializes in fabric and paper projects and enjoys combining new materials with vintage or repurposed finds. Her work has been published in numerous books and magazines, and she blogs at www.kirstyneale.typepad.com

06

07

CUTE CROCHET

FOREST FRIENDS

THESE FINGER PUPPETS FEATURE FIVE DIFFERENT WOODLAND CHARACTERS WITH INDIVIDUALLY CROCHETED FEATURES FOR EXTRA EXPRESSION. MADE IN THE SOFTEST ALPACA YARN IN RUSTIC COLORS, EACH PUPPET IS ABOUT 3⅛" (8 cm) HIGH AND 1½" (3.8 cm) WIDE WHEN LAID FLAT.

FIVE FUN
FINGER
PUPPETS

HOW TO MAKE ... FOREST FRIENDS

MATERIALS

50G BALLS (183 YARDS/167 METERS) OF DROPS ALPACA, ONE IN EACH OF BROWN 401 (A), LIGHT BROWN 607 (B), BLACK 8903 (C), OFF-WHITE 100 (D), MEDIUM GRAY 517 (E), MAROON 3650 (F), RUST 2925 (G), CAMEL BEIGE 302 (H), AND OLIVE 7233 (I), OR SIMILAR (SPORT-WEIGHT 100% ALPACA)

SIZE B1 OR C2 (2.5MM) CROCHET HOOK

STITCH MARKER

TEN BLACK SEED BEADS FOR EYES

BLACK SEWING THREAD

SEWING NEEDLE

TAPESTRY NEEDLE

TENSION TIP

Achieving a suggested tension is not important for this project.

01 Start bear and moose bodies.
All sc sts are made into back loop only of previous sc round; this creates a ridged effect.
Foundation round: Using yarn A for bear and B for moose, make 18ch and sl st to join round.
Round 1: 1sc in each ch. (18sc)
Rounds 2–16: 1sc in each sc.
Add details to the faces before dec and completing the bodies.

02 Add details to bear and moose faces.
Make the muzzles:
Round 1: Using yarn B for both animals, make a magic loop, make 5sc into loop, draw the circle closed and join with sl st.
Round 2: 2sc in each sc, join round with sl st. (10sc)
Fasten off and weave in ends. Sew to face.
Make the bear's nose:
Using yarn C, make 2ch loosely. Yarn over hook, insert hook into second ch from hook, pull yarn through so you have 3 loops on hook. Yarn over hook and pull through latest loop. Rep until you have 7 loops on hook. Carefully pull yarn through all loops on hook. Insert hook into second ch of foundation ch and make 1sc. Fasten off. Using the end of your

hook, push yarn ends into the middle of the bobble (this rounds out the nose shape and hides the yarn ends). Sew nose to muzzle.
Make the moose's nose:
Embroider two black points to the moose's muzzle to form nostrils.
Make the eyes:
Using yarn D, embroider two small circles to form the whites of the eyes. Sew on two black seed beads for the pupils.

03 Complete bear and moose bodies.
Round 17: 1sc in 2sc, sc2tog, [1sc, sc2tog] four times, 1sc in last 2sc. (13sc)
Round 18: [1sc, sc2tog] four times, 1sc in last sc. (9sc)
Round 19: Sl st in first sc, [sc2tog] four times. (4sc)
Round 20: Skip 3sc, 1sc in last sc. (1sc).
Thread yarn end through rem st to fasten off. Weave in ends.

04 Make bear's ears (make 2).
Round 1: Using yarn C, make a magic loop, work 7sc into loop, draw the circle closed and join with sl st.
Round 2: Fasten off yarn C and join yarn A. 2sc in each sc, sl st to join round. (14sc)
Fasten off. Rep for second ear. Fasten off and weave in ends. Sew ears to bear's head.

05 Make moose's antlers (make 2).
Foundation chain: Using yarn C, make 10ch.

First branch: Sl st into first 4ch of foundation ch.

Second branch: Make 4ch, sl st into first 3ch of 4ch, sl st into fifth ch of foundation ch.

Third branch: Make 4ch, sl st into first 3ch of 4ch, sl st into sixth ch of foundation ch. Sl st into rem ch of foundation ch.

Rep for second antler. Fasten off and sew antlers to moose's head.

06 Make moose's ears (make 2). Attach yarn B to top side of head, make 3ch.

Row 1: 1sc in second ch from hook, 1sc in final ch, sl st to join

to side of head, fasten off. Rep for second ear. Fasten off and weave in ends.

07 Start rabbit and fox bodies. All sc sts are made into back loop only of previous sc round; this creates a ridged effect.

Foundation round: Using yarn E for rabbit and F for fox, make 18ch and sl st to join round.

Round 1: 1sc in each ch. (18sc)
Rounds 2–11: 1sc in each sc.
Round 12: 1sc in first 3sc, join yarn D (do not break main color yarn), 1sc in next 3sc, change back to main color yarn, complete round.
Rounds 13–14: 1sc in first sc, pick up yarn D, 1sc in next 5sc, change back to main color, complete round.
Round 15: As round 12.
Round 16: As round 11.
Add details to the faces before dec and completing the bodies.

08 Add details to rabbit and fox faces. Make the noses:
As bear's nose, step 2.
Make the mouth:
For rabbit only, embroider three lines for mouth using black sewing thread.
Make the eyes:
As step 2.

09 Complete rabbit and fox bodies. As step 3.

10 Make fox's ears (make 2). Attach yarn D to side of fox's head.

DESIGNED BY OLIVIA KOVACS

Row 1: Working into sts at top of fox's head, 1sc in next 3 sts, turn. (3sc)
Row 2: 1ch, 1sc into each sc, turn.
Row 3: 1ch, skip 2sc, 1sc into final sc. (1sc)
Row 4: Thread yarn through rem st, and fasten off. Join yarn F, work 1sc evenly around the sts of inner ear. Join with sl st to head and fasten off. Rep on other side of head for second ear. Fasten off and weave in ends.

11 Make rabbit's ears (make 2).
Foundation row: Using yarn D, make 8ch (5ch for foundation row plus 3ch counts as 1dc).
Row 1: 1dc in fourth ch from hook, 1dc in next 2ch, 1sc in rem 2ch. (6 sts)
Round 2: Fasten off yarn D, join yarn E. Make 2sc in each st, 2sc in sp between 3ch and next st, then, working into other side of foundation ch, 2sc in each ch. Join with sl st and fasten off. Weave in ends. Rep for second ear. Stitch ears to rabbit's face. Fasten off and weave in ends.

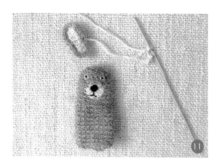

12 Start squirrel body.
All sc sts are made into back loop only of previous sc round; this creates a ridged effect.
Foundation round: Using yarn G, make 18ch and sl st to join round.
Round 1: Work 1sc in first 7ch, join yarn D, make 1sc in next 4ch, pick up yarn G and complete round.
Rounds 2–14: Work 1sc in next 7sc, join yarn D, make 1sc in next 4sc, pick up yarn G and complete round.
Round 15: Work 1sc in first 8sc, join yarn D, make 1sc in next 2sc, pick up yarn G and complete round.
Round 16: Using yarn G, 1sc in each sc.
Add details to the faces before dec and completing the bodies.

13 Add details to squirrel's face.
Make the nose:
As bear's nose, step 2.
Make the eyes:
As step 2.

14 Complete squirrel body.
As step 3.

15 Make squirrel's ears (make 2).
Join yarn G to top of squirrel's head, make 4ch.
Row 1: 1sc in second ch from hook, 1sc in rem 2ch, sl st to join to head. Fasten off. Rep for second ear. Fasten off and weave in ends.

16 Make squirrel's front paws (make 2).
Join yarn G to side of squirrel's body, make 12ch (9ch for foundation ch plus 3ch counts as 1dc).
Row 1: 1dc in fourth ch from hook, 1dc in rem ch. (10dc)
Sl st to join to body. Fasten off. Rep for other paw. Fasten off and weave in ends.

17 Make squirrel's acorn.
Round 1: Using yarn H, make a magic loop, make 5sc into loop, draw circle closed and join with sl st.
Round 2: 2sc in each sc. (10sc).
Round 3: Fasten off yarn H and join yarn I. Work decs [skip 1sc, 1sc in next sc] until you have run out of sts. Sl st to join. Fasten off, leaving long yarn ends. Using the end of your hook, push the yarn ends into the inside of the acorn to stuff it slightly. Sew one paw to each side of the acorn. Fasten off and weave in ends.

WORKING THE STITCHES

FOLLOW THE INSTRUCTIONS FOR WORKING THE HAND EMBROIDERY STITCHES USED FOR THE BOOK'S MAKES.

Cross stitch

Starting a thread: knot the long end of the wool; insert needle through the front of your work a few holes away in the direction you will be stitching; when you reach the knot, snip it off.

Working cross stitch: method 1
Working left to right, make a row of diagonal stitches. Up at 1, down at 2, up at 3. Repeat. Working right to left, complete the Xs with a row of diagonal stitches. Up at 4, down at 5, up at 6. Repeat.

Working cross stitch: method 2
Work left to right. Up at 1, down at 2, up at 3. Down at 4, up at 5. Repeat.

Finishing a thread
Slide the needle through five to six stitches on the back of your work to secure and finish off the thread.

Running stitch

Work right to left. Up at 1, down at 2. Up at 3, down at 4. Repeat.

Backstitch

Work right to left. Up at 1, down at 2. Up at 3, down at 4. Repeat.

Chain stitch

Work right to left. Up at 1, down at 1, keeping thread in a small loop. Up at 2, down at 2, keeping thread in a small loop. Repeat.

French knot

Up at 1. Wrap thread around needle two times. Down at 2, holding thread taut around needle while pulling through.

Satin stitch

Up at 1. Down at 2, up at 3. Down at 4. Repeat, working across the area you are filling.

Blanket stitch

Start by coming up at the edge. Down at 1. Up at 2 under fabric edge, keeping needle over working thread. Repeat.

TEMPLATES

HERE ARE ALL THE SHAPES FOR THE BOOK'S PROJECTS. ENLARGE ALL TEMPLATES BY 200% BY PHOTOCOPYING THE PAGES, WITH THE EXCEPTION OF SILVER LEAF GARLAND, HEDGEHOG SEWING SET, ANIMAL PICTURES, FOXY SLEEP MASK, AND STAG HEAD, WHICH SHOULD BE ENLARGED BY 400%. YOU CAN ALSO FIND THE FULL-SIZE TEMPLATES READY TO DOWNLOAD FROM WWW.LOVECRAFTS.CO.UK.

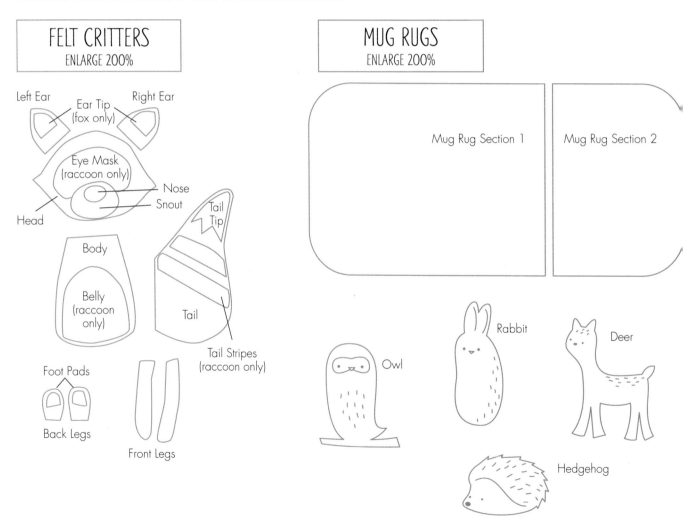

FELT CRITTERS
ENLARGE 200%

Left Ear · Ear Tip (fox only) · Right Ear

Eye Mask (raccoon only)

Head · Nose · Snout

Body

Belly (raccoon only)

Tail Tip · Tail · Tail Stripes (raccoon only)

Foot Pads · Back Legs

Front Legs

MUG RUGS
ENLARGE 200%

Mug Rug Section 1 · Mug Rug Section 2

Owl · Rabbit · Deer · Hedgehog

SILVER LEAF GARLAND
ENLARGE 400%

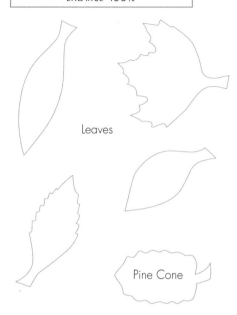

Leaves

Pine Cone

HEDGEHOG SEWING SET
ENLARGE 400%

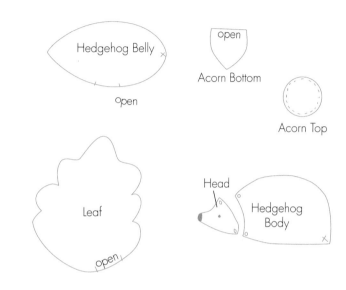

Hedgehog Belly

Open

open

Acorn Bottom

Acorn Top

Leaf

open

Head

Hedgehog Body

ANIMAL PICTURES
ENLARGE 400%

Squirrel

Mouse

Fawn

FOXY SLEEP MASK
ENLARGE 400%

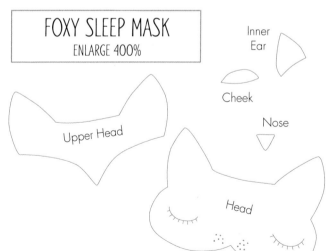

Inner Ear

Cheek

Nose

Upper Head

Head

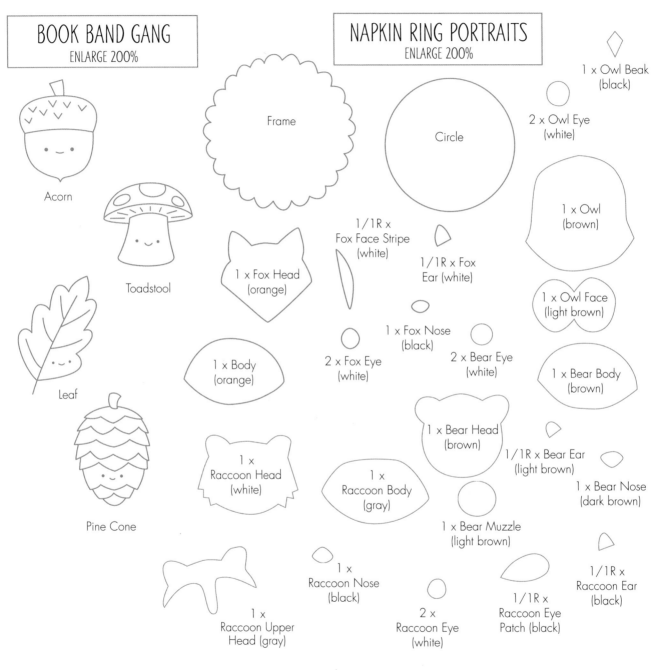

BOOK BAND GANG
ENLARGE 200%

Acorn

Toadstool

Leaf

Pine Cone

NAPKIN RING PORTRAITS
ENLARGE 200%

Frame

Circle

1 x Owl Beak
(black)

2 x Owl Eye
(white)

1 x Owl
(brown)

1 x Owl Face
(light brown)

1 x Fox Head
(orange)

1/1R x
Fox Face Stripe
(white)

1/1R x Fox
Ear (white)

1 x Fox Nose
(black)

2 x Fox Eye
(white)

2 x Bear Eye
(white)

1 x Bear Body
(brown)

1 x Body
(orange)

1 x Bear Head
(brown)

1/1R x Bear Ear
(light brown)

1 x Bear Nose
(dark brown)

1 x
Raccoon Head
(white)

1 x
Raccoon Body
(gray)

1 x Bear Muzzle
(light brown)

1 x
Raccoon Nose
(black)

1 x
Raccoon Upper
Head (gray)

2 x
Raccoon Eye
(white)

1/1R x
Raccoon Eye
Patch (black)

1/1R x
Raccoon Ear
(black)

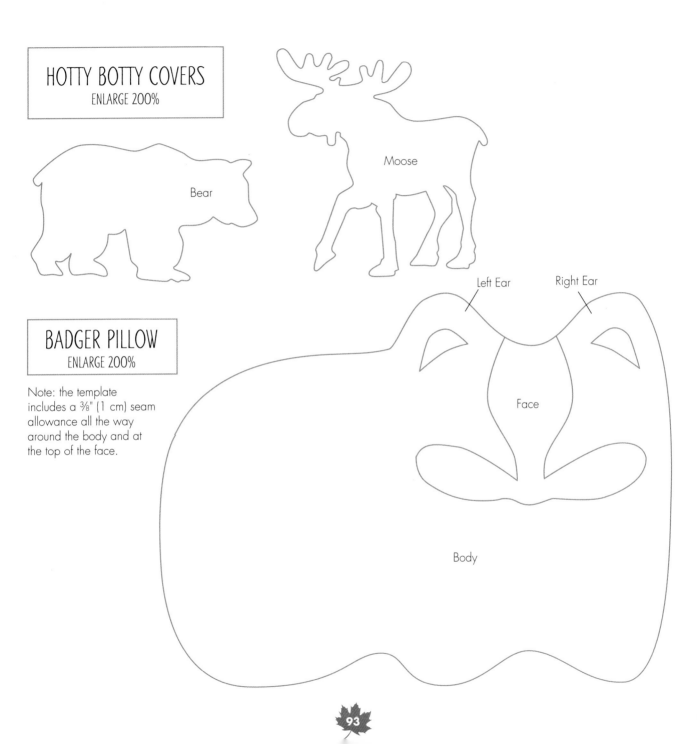

HOTTY BOTTY COVERS
ENLARGE 200%

Bear

Moose

BADGER PILLOW
ENLARGE 200%

Note: the template
includes a ⅜" (1 cm) seam
allowance all the way
around the body and at
the top of the face.

Left Ear

Right Ear

Face

Body

STAG HEAD
ENLARGE 400%

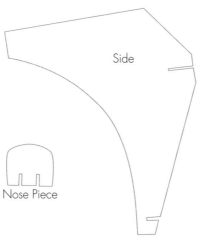

Side

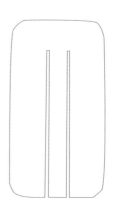

Nose Piece

Backing
(note: cut 1 with slots and 1 without slots)

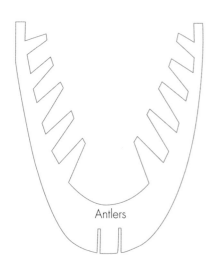

Antlers

HAPPY LOG POUCH
ENLARGE 200%

Embroidery Pattern

CHARTS

SQUIRREL HAND WARMERS

Acorn

Squirrel

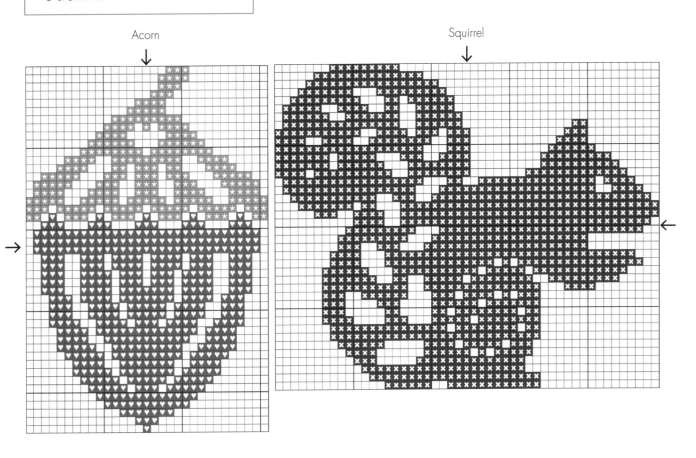

Key

 ♥ ■ Anchor 370/DMC 975

★ ■ Anchor 365/DMC 3826

Key

✖ ■ Anchor 351/DMC 400

DISCOVER MORE MOLLIE MAKES TITLES
available from Interweave

MOLLIE MAKES CHRISTMAS
Living and Loving a Handmade Holiday
ISBN 978-1-62033-101-9 | $12.95

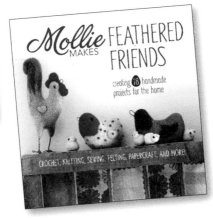

MOLLIE MAKES FEATHERED FRIENDS
Creating 18 Handmade Projects for the Home
ISBN 978-1-59668-775-2 | $12.95

MOLLIE MAKES CROCHET
20+ Cute Projects for the Home
Plus Handy Tips and Tricks
ISBN 978-1-62033-095-1 | $19.95

For more information on *Mollie Makes*, please visit molliemakes.com

First published in the United States in 2013 by Interweave
A division of F+W Media, Inc.
201 East Fourth Street
Loveland, CO 80537
interweave.com

ISBN 978-1-62033-540-6

Library of Congress Cataloging-in-Publication Data not available at time of printing.

10 9 8 7 6 5 4 3 2 1

Manufactured in China by 1010.

PUBLISHER'S ACKNOWLEDGMENTS

This book would not have been possible without the input of all our crafty contributors, who have provided all our brilliant how-to projects and step-by-step photography. We would also like to thank Cheryl Brown, who has done an excellent job of pulling everything together, and Sophie Martin for her design layout. Thanks to Mollie Johanson for allowing us to use her stitch diagrams. Main project photography by Rachel Whiting.

And of course, thanks must go to the fantastic team at *Mollie Makes* for all their help, in particular Lara Watson, Jane Toft, and Katherine Ra

31232009785843